CONTENTS

PREFACE

This is the latest in a long line of Hugo phrase books and is of excellent pedigree, having been compiled by experts to meet the general needs of tourists and business travellers. Arranged under the usual headings of 'Hotels', 'Motoring' and so forth, the ample selection of useful words and phrases is supported by a 1,900-line Mini-Dictionary to help you form additional phrases (or at least express the one word you need!). There's also a Menu Reader which will ease your way through some 250 food items, dishes and culinary terms. The Hebrew words and phrases you may need are also printed in familiar roman letters following an easy-to-use pronunciation system that is fully explained on page 5. You should have no difficulty reading the phrases, but if you use our audio-cassette of selected extracts from the book, then you should be word-perfect! Ask your bookseller for the Hugo Hebrew Travel Pack.

Of course you will want to know what various signs and notices mean when they are written in Hebrew; there are lists of common signs (pages 15-17) and road signs (pages 31-2), as well as recognition boxes headed *Things you'll see* in most sections of the book. These cover words, signs, notices, etc.

Guidance on the Israeli way of life, manners, customs and holidays will be found under the heading *Cross-Cultural Notes*; an understanding of such matters will greatly enhance your trip and understanding of Israeli culture.

INTRODUCTION

PRONUNCIATION

When reading the imitated pronunciation, stress that part which is underlined. Pronounce each syllable as if it formed part of an English word, and you will be understood sufficiently well. Remember the points below, and your pronunciation will be even closer to the correct Hebrew:

ai	as in 'Thai'
ay	as in 'pay'
e	as in 'bed'
er	as in 'where'
g	as in 'good'
KH	'ch' as in the Scottish word 'loch'
o	as in 'hot' (remember that words such as **lo** are not pronounced 'low')
u	as in 'pull'
ZH	's' as in 'leisure'
'	signifies a guttural, 'throaty' sound at the start of the next syllable

The mini-dictionary provides the Hebrew translations using the imitated pronunciation so that you can read the words without reference to the Hebrew alphabet. The abbreviations *(m)* and *(f)* used in this book indicate the forms to be used by a male or female speaker or, in the case of an adjective, the forms to be used when referring to a male or female. All Hebrew adjectives have masculine, feminine and plural forms but, except for adjectives describing people, the dictionary shows the masculine forms. The forms to be used when speaking to a man or a woman are indicated by *(to a man)* and *(to a woman)* following the words applying to each.

Hebrew has no vowels and only an experienced reader can know whether the written character is pronounced with a, e, i, o, or u. You may sometimes come across texts - the Hebrew Bible, for example, as well as children's books - which have a vowel system

consisting of dots and lines, called **nikud** (punctuation marks). However, most of the everyday written Hebrew that you will encounter will not have vowel sounds shown.

'The' in Hebrew is **ha-** added to the beginning of the noun and also to the beginning of both the adjective and the noun when both are used. There is no indefinite article (a, an) in Hebrew.

THE HEBREW ALPHABET

The first letter of the alphabet, א, is the equivalent of the English letter 'a', but it can be pronounced in any of the following ways:

a   as in 'arm'
e   as in 'elf'
i   as in 'inn'
o   as in 'order'
oo as in 'ooze'

Most other letters used in this book have direct equivalents in the English alphabet:

א	a (also e, i, etc see above)
ב	b or v
ג	g as in 'good'
ד	d
ה	h
ו	v or o as in 'hot' or u as in 'pull'
ז	z
ח	KH like 'ch' in 'loch'
ט	t
י	y or i
כ	KH like 'ch' in 'loch' or k
ל	l
מ	m
נ	n
ס	s
ע	pronounced like א but from the back of the throat
פ	p or f
צ	tz as in 'Ritz'

6

ק   k
ר   r
ש   sh as in 'shop', but sometimes pronounced s
ת   t

The following letters have a different form (but the same sound) when appearing at the end of a word:

letter	end of word form	
כ	ך	KH
מ	ם	m
נ	ן	n
פ	ף	f
צ	ץ	tz

Although the following do not appear in this book, you might see them occasionally:

וּ   u as in 'pull'
וֹ   o as in 'hot'
כּ   k
בּ   b
פּ   p

CROSS-CULTURAL NOTES

Many aspects of Israeli society can appear, to a first-time visitor, surprisingly Western. In terms of technology, communications and everyday facilities Israel resembles European countries. Tel Aviv is a modern, bustling metropolis, where art, theatre and cinema are thriving. Jerusalem displays a far more complex picture: it is a fascinating mixture of old and new, with traditional Arab and orthodox Jewish neighbourhoods maintaining a tense coexistence alongside the secular, modern parts of the city. The kibbutzim (plural of 'kibbutz', a communal settlement) and the moshavim (communal villages) are interesting social experiments, combining socialist and liberal values, and based upon modern farming and industry.

Most Israelis, regardless of their ethnic or political affiliations, are friendly, informal and talkative. Many speak some English, but would be delighted to hear your Hebrew. You'll find that, even with strangers, on public transport and in shops, for example, Israelis do not stand on ceremony. Physical gestures are more common than in northern Europe. First names are universally used, except in extremely formal situations. A great deal can be done without a jacket or a tie, and dress is usually casual and well-adapted to the climate. There are few inhibitions in conversation: even total strangers would not hesitate to embark on a political discussion. Your views may be vehemently contested, but you are welcome to put them forward. Personal matters are discussed more freely than in Britain, though less than in the US.

Despite this openness, tact and common sense are recommended when encountering the sensitive areas of Israeli society: the Jewish majority originates from over a hundred countries, from Poland to Ethiopia. It is extremely varied in its lifestyle, attitude to religion, and political outlook. Israel's Muslim and Christian Arabs (some 18% of the population), and the Palestinians living in the occupied West Bank and Gaza Strip, again display a variety of customs and opinions. It would be useful to acquaint yourself with the current state of debate on the Israeli-Arab conflict. Generally speaking, the Israeli Left has traditionally supported a territorial compromise and

more attention to civil rights, while the Right is more concerned with the value of the occupied territories for Israel's security and its Jewish cultural-religious identity.

Israel itself is, on the whole, safe for travellers and tourists but not all parts of Jerusalem or Israel's occupied territories are equally safe. For women, modest dress is advisable in the Arab areas and in the orthodox Jewish neighbourhoods.

Israel's religious establishment is politically more powerful than most of its Western counterparts, even though most Israelis are avowedly secular. The religion's mark on everyday life is most noticeable with regard to the Sabbath and the Jewish dietary rules. The Jewish Sabbath lasts from Friday afternoon to early Saturday evening. Public transport is very limited at this time: banks, shops and some restaurants are closed and it's advisable to seek advice locally and plan accordingly. However, in most areas theatres, cinemas, restaurants and cafés remain open.

Kosher dietary rules apply in many restaurants and most hotels. Basically, this means that meat and milk products cannot be eaten together, that pork and shellfish are not served, and that your hotel will serve a cold buffet on Saturday. Alcoholic drinks are available – Israel produces its own wine and beers, but their consumption is far less central to social life than in Britain. To Israelis, a 'drink' is most likely to mean a soft drink, unless 'alcoholic' is explicitly stated.

THE JEWISH CALENDAR

Although the Jewish calendar varies by a few days each year, the broad pattern is the same: Av is July/August, Elul is August/September etc.

JEWISH MONTHS

Tishrei	תשרי	tishray
Heshvan	חשון	KHeshvan
Kislev	כסלו	kislev
Teveth	טבת	tevet
Shevat	שבט	shvat

Adar*	אדר	adar
Nisan	ניסן	nisan
Iyar	אייר	iyar
Sivan	סיון	sivan
Tammuz	תמוז	tamuz
Av	אב	av
Elul	אלול	elul

* Every few years, a thirteenth month, **Adar Bet** is added between Adar and Nisan to adjust the Jewish year to the general calendar.

JEWISH FESTIVALS

Jewish New Year ראש השנה rosh ha-shana
— literally 'head of the year', 1 and 2 Tishrei (in September or October)

Yom Kippur יום כפור yom kipur
— means 'the Day of Atonement' on 10 Tishrei (usually in October)

Feast of Tabernacles סוכות sukot
— 15-21 Tishrei (usually in October)

Hanukah חנוכה KHanuka
— commemorates the victory of the Maccabees and falls around Christmas time

Tu B'Shevat טו בשבט tu b'shvat
— literally 'the New Year of Trees', celebrating the first signs of spring

Purim פורים purim
— festival of rejoicing associated with the book of Esther and relating to the Jewish exile in Persia, usually in March

Passover פסח pesaKH
— 15-21 Nisan, around Easter time

Memorial Day יום הזכרון yom ha-zikaron
— Day of Remembrance, preceding Independence Day

Independence Day יום העצמאות yom ha-'atzma'ut
— usually in April or May

Feast of Weeks שבועות shavu'ot
— harvest festival, usually in May or June

Fast of Av תשעה באב tish'a be-'av
— commemorates the Destruction of the Jewish Temple, usually in August

USEFUL EVERYDAY PHRASES

Yes/no
כן/לא
ken/lo

Thank you
תודה
to<u>da</u>

No thank you
לא תודה
lo to<u>da</u>

Please
בבקשה
bevaka<u>sha</u>

I don't understand
אני לא מבין/מבינה
a<u>ni</u> lo me<u>vin</u> (m)/mevi<u>na</u> (f)

Do you speak English/French/German?
אתה מדבר אנגלית/צרפתית/גרמנית?
a<u>ta</u> meda<u>ber</u> ang<u>lit</u>/tzorfa<u>tit</u>/germa<u>nit</u>? (to a man)

את מדברת אנגלית/צרפתית/גרמנית?
at medabe<u>ret</u> ang<u>lit</u>/tzorfa<u>tit</u>/germa<u>nit</u>? (to a woman)

I can't speak Hebrew
אני לא מדבר/מדברת עברית
a<u>ni</u> lo meda<u>ber</u> (m)/medabe<u>ret</u> (f) iv<u>rit</u>

I don't know
אני לא יודע/יודעת
a<u>ni</u> lo yode'a (m)/yoda'at (f)

Please speak more slowly
בבקשה לדבר יותר לאט
bevaka<u>sha</u> leda<u>ber</u> yo<u>ter</u> le<u>'at</u>

Please write it down for me
בבקשה לכתוב את זה בשבילי
bevaka<u>sha</u> liKH<u>tov</u> et zeh bishvi<u>li</u>

My name is ...
... שמי
shmi ...

Pleased to meet you
נעים מאד
na<u>'im</u> me<u>od</u>

Good morning
בקר טוב
<u>bo</u>ker tov

Good evening
ערב טוב
<u>e</u>rev tov

Good night
לילה טוב
<u>lai</u>la tov

Goodbye
שלום
sha<u>lom</u>

See you later
להתראות
lehitra<u>'ot</u>

12

How are you?
מה שלומך?
ma shlomKHa? *(to a man)*

מה שלומך?
ma shlomeKH? *(to a woman)*

Excuse me please
סליחה בבקשה
sliKHa bevakasha

Sorry!
סליחה!
sliKHa!

I'm really sorry
אני מאד מצטער/מצטערת
ani meod mitzta'er *(m)*/mitzta'eret *(f)*

Can you help me?
אפשר לעזור לי?
efshar la'azor li?

Can you tell me ...?
אפשר להגיד לי ...?
efshar lehagid li ...?

Can I have ...?
אפשר לקבל ...?
efshar lekabel ...?

Is there ... here?
האם יש ... כאן?
ha'im yesh ... kan?

Where can I get ...?
איפה אפשר להשיג ?
ayfo efshar lehasig ...?

13

USEFUL EVERYDAY PHRASES

How much is it?
כמה זה עולה?
<u>ka</u>ma zeh o<u>leh</u>?

What time is it?
מה השעה?
ma ha-sha<u>'a</u>?

I must go now
אני צריך/צריכה ללכת עכשיו
<u>a</u>ni tzari<u>KH</u> *(m)*/tzri<u>KH</u>a *(f)* lale<u>KH</u>et a<u>KH</u>shav

I'm lost
הלכתי לאיבוד
hala<u>KH</u>ti le'i<u>bud</u>

Cheers!
לחיים!
le-<u>KH</u>ayim!

Do you take credit cards?
אתם מקבלים כרטיסי אשראי?
<u>a</u>tem meka<u>blim</u> karti<u>say</u> ash<u>rai</u>?

Where is the toilet?
איפה השירותים?
<u>ay</u>fo ha-sheru<u>tim</u>?

Go away!
לך מפה!
le<u>KH</u> mi-<u>po</u>!

Excellent!
מצויין!
metzu<u>yan</u>!

14

THINGS YOU'LL HEAR

ani lo mev<u>i</u>n *(m)*/**mevin<u>a</u>** *(f)*	I don't understand
<u>a</u>ni lo yod<u>e</u>ʿa *(m)*/**yod<u>a</u>ʿat** *(f)*	I don't know
be-ʿemet?	Really?; Is that so?
bevak<u>a</u>sha	You're welcome; please
im yirtz<u>e</u>h ha-sh<u>e</u>m	God willing
lehitraʿot	See you later
ma nish<u>ma</u>?	How's it going?
ma shlom<u>KHA</u>? *(to a man)*	How are you?
ma shlome<u>KH</u>? *(to a woman)*	How are you?
na<u>KH</u>on	That's right
r<u>e</u>ga e<u>KH</u>ad!	Just a minute!
shab<u>a</u>t shal<u>o</u>m	Good Sabbath *(said on Friday evening and Saturday)*
shal<u>o</u>m	Goodbye
shal<u>o</u>m, naʿim me<u>o</u>d	Hello, pleased to meet you
shav<u>u</u>ʿa tov	Have a good week *(said on Saturday night)*
sli<u>KH</u>a?	Pardon?
to<u>da</u>	Thanks
tov to<u>da</u> ve-<u>a</u>ta? *(to a man)*	Very well thank you – and you?
tov to<u>da</u> ve-at? *(to a woman)*	Very well thank you – and you?
zeh lo meshan<u>e</u>	It doesn't matter
zehir<u>u</u>t!	Be careful!

THINGS YOU'LL SEE

הכניסה חינם	**ha-knisa KHinam**	admission free
חוף הים	**KHof ha-y<u>a</u>m**	beach
באר שבע	**be'<u>e</u>r sh<u>e</u>va**	Beersheba
קופה	**kupa**	cash desk

→

15

כנסיה	**knesiya**	church
מרכז העיר	**merkaz ha‘ir**	city centre
סגור	**sagur**	closed
סגור לתקופת החגים	**sagur le-tekufat ha-KHagim**	closed for the holiday period
הנחה	**hanaKHa**	discount
מי שתיה	**may shtiya**	drinking water
אילת	**aylat**	Eilat
יציאת חרום	**yetzi‘at KHerum**	emergency exit
תפוס	**tafus**	engaged, reserved
דירה להשכרה	**dira le-haskara**	flat for rent
אסור	**asur**	forbidden
למכירה	**le-meKHira**	for sale
גברים	**gvarim**	gentlemen
חיפה	**KHaifa**	Haifa
צ.ה.ל.	**tzahal**	Israeli Defence Forces
ירושלים	**yerushalayim**	Jerusalem
כשר	**kasher**	kosher
נשים	**nashim**	ladies
מעלית	**ma‘alit**	lift
שטח צבאי	**shetaKH tzva‘i**	military zone
מסגד	**misgad**	mosque
הכניסה אסורה	**ha-knisa asurah**	no admission
אין כניסה	**ayn knisa**	no entry
העיר העתיקה	**ha-‘ir ha-atika**	old city
פתוח	**patuaKH**	open
פרטי	**prati**	private
משוך	**meshoKH**	pull
דחוף	**deKHof**	push
עתיקות	**atikot**	ruins, antiques
מבצע, מכירה	**mivtza, meKHira**	sale
שקט	**sheket**	silence, quiet
חפץ חשוד	**KHefetz KHashud**	suspicious object
בית כנסת	**bayt kneset**	synagogue

→

תל אביב	tel a<u>viv</u>	Tel Aviv
שירותים	sheru<u>tim</u>	toilets
פנוי	pa<u>nui</u>	vacant
שעות ביקור	she'ot bi<u>kur</u>	visiting hours
כניסה	k<u>nisa</u>	way in, entrance
יציאה	yetzi'<u>a</u>	way out, exit
צבע טרי	<u>tze</u>va ta<u>ri</u>	wet paint

DAYS, MONTHS, SEASONS

Sunday	יום ראשון	yom rishon
Monday	יום שני	yom sheni
Tuesday	יום שלישי	yom shlishi
Wednesday	יום רביעי	yom revi'i
Thursday	יום חמישי	yom KHamishi
Friday	יום שישי	yom shishi
Saturday	שבת	shabat

January	ינואר	yanuar
February	פברואר	februar
March	מרס, מרץ	mars, mertz
April	אפריל	april
May	מאי	mai
June	יוני	yuni
July	יולי	yuli
August	אוגוסט	ogust
September	ספטמבר	september
October	אוקטובר	oktober
November	נובמבר	november
December	דצמבר	detzember

Spring	אביב	aviv
Summer	קיץ	kayitz
Autumn	סתו	stav
Winter	חורף	KHoref

Christmas Eve	ערב חג המולד	erev KHag ha-molad
Christmas	חג המולד	KHag ha-molad
New Year's Eve	ערב ראש השנה האזרחית	erev rosh ha-shana ha-ezraKHit
New Year's Day	ראש השנה האזרחית	rosh ha-shana ha-ezraKHit
Easter	חג הפסחא	KHag ha-pasKHa
Ramadan (Muslim month of fasting)	רמדן	ramadan

18

NUMBERS

The numbers below are given in the feminine form. This is the form you are most likely to need since it is used for counting and telling the time.

0	אפס	efes
1	אחת	aKHat
2	שתיים	shtayim
3	שלוש	shalosh
4	ארבע	arba
5	חמש	KHamesh
6	שש	shesh
7	שבע	sheva
8	שמונה	shmoneh
9	תשע	tesha
10	עשר	eser
11	אחת עשרה	aKHat esreh
12	שתים עשרה	shtaym esreh
13	שלוש עשרה	shlosh esreh
14	ארבע עשרה	arba esreh
15	חמש עשרה	KHamesh esreh
16	שש עשרה	shesh esreh
17	שבע עשרה	shva esreh
18	שמונה עשרה	shmoneh esreh
19	תשע עשרה	tesha esreh
20	עשרים	esrim
21	עשרים ואחת	esrim ve-aKHat
22	עשרים ושתיים	esrim ve-shtayim
30	שלושים	shloshim
31	שלושים ואחת	shloshim ve-aKHat
40	ארבעים	arba'im
50	חמישים	KHamishim
60	שישים	shishim
70	שבעים	shiv'im
80	שמונים	shmonim

90	תשעים	tish'im
100	מאה	me'a
110	מאה ועשר	me'a ve-'eser
200	מאתיים	matayim
300	שלוש מאות	shlosh me'ot
400	ארבע מאות	arba me'ot
500	חמש מאות	KHamesh me'ot
600	שש מאות	shesh me'ot
700	שבע מאות	shva me'ot
800	שמונה מאות	shmoneh me'ot
900	תשע מאות	tesha me'ot
1,000	אלף	elef
10,000	עשרת אלפים	aseret alafim
20,000	עשרים אלף	esrim elef
100,000	מאה אלף	me'a elef
1,000,000	מיליון	milion

TIME

today	היום	hayom
yesterday	אתמול	etmol
tomorrow	מחר	maKHar
the day before yesterday	שלשום	shilshom
the day after tomorrow	מחרתיים	moKHrotayim
this week	השבוע	ha-shavu'a
last week	השבוע שעבר	ha-shavu'a she-'avar
next week	השבוע הבא	ha-shavu'a ha-ba
this morning	הבוקר	ha-boker
this afternoon	אחר הצהריים	aKHar ha-tzohorayim
this evening	הערב	ha-erev
tonight	הלילה	ha-laila
yesterday afternoon	אתמול אחר הצהריים	etmol aKHar ha-tzohorayim
last night	אמש	emesh
tomorrow morning	מחר בבוקר	maKHar ba-boker
tomorrow evening	מחר בערב	maKHar ba-erev
in three days	עוד שלושה ימים	od shlosha yamim

TIME

three days ago	לפני שלושה ימים	lifnay shlo<u>sh</u>a yamim
late	מאוחר	me'u<u>KH</u>ar
early	מוקדם	mukdam
soon	בקרוב	bekarov
later on	אחר כך	a<u>KH</u>ar ka<u>KH</u>
at the moment	כרגע	karega
second	שניה	shniya
minute	דקה	daka
one minute	דקה אחת	daka a<u>KH</u>at
two minutes	שתי דקות	shtay <u>d</u>akot
quarter of an hour	רבע שעה	reva sha'a
half an hour	חצי שעה	<u>KH</u>atzi sha'a
three quarters of an hour	שלושת רבעי שעה	shloshet riv'<u>ay</u> sha'a
hour	שעה	sha'a
that day	אותו היום	oto ha-<u>yom</u>
every day	כל יום	kol yom
all day	כל היום	kol ha-<u>yom</u>
the next day	למחרת	lemo<u>KH</u>o<u>rat</u>

TELLING THE TIME

'It's ... o'clock' in Hebrew is **ha-sha'a ...**, followed by the number of the hour. 'It's two o'clock' is therefore **ha-sha'a shtayim**. 'Quarter past' is **va-<u>reva</u>**, so 'quarter past two' is **shtayim va-<u>reva</u>**. 'Half past' is **va-<u>KH</u>etzi**, so 'half past two' is **shtayim va-<u>KH</u>etzi**. 'Quarter to' is **<u>reva</u> le-...**, so 'quarter to three' is **<u>reva</u> le-shalosh**. Any number of minutes after two o'clock would be **shtayim ve-... dakot**. Any number of minutes (if it is less than thirty) before three o'clock would be **... dakot le-shalosh**. The twenty-four hour clock is used mostly for military purposes. To distinguish between a.m. and p.m., it's possible to use the words 'in the morning' **ba-<u>boker</u>**, 'in the afternoon' **ba-tzoho<u>rayim</u>** or **a<u>KH</u>aray ha-tzoho<u>rayim</u>**, 'in the evening' **ba-erev** or 'at night' **ba-laila**. Thus, '7 a.m.' would be **<u>sheva</u> ba-<u>boker</u>**, and '4 p.m.' – **<u>arba</u> a<u>KH</u>aray ha-tzoho<u>rayim</u>**.

TIME

a.m.	בבוקר	ba-<u>bo</u>ker
p.m. *(afternoon)*	בצהריים,	ba-<u>tzoho</u>rayim,
	אחרי הצהריים	a<u>KHaray</u>
		ha-<u>tzoho</u>rayim
(evening)	בערב	ba-<u>e</u>rev
one o'clock	אחת	a<u>KHat</u>
ten past one	אחת ועשרה	a<u>KHat</u> va-'a<u>sa</u>ra
quarter past one	אחת ורבע	a<u>KHat</u> va-<u>re</u>va
half past one	אחת וחצי	a<u>KHat</u> va-<u>KHe</u>tzi
twenty to two	עשרים לשתים	es<u>rim</u> le-<u>shta</u>yim
quarter to two	רבע לשתים	<u>re</u>va le-<u>shta</u>yim
two o'clock	שתים	<u>shta</u>yim
13.00	אחת	a<u>KHat</u>
16.30	ארבע וחצי	<u>ar</u>ba va-<u>KHe</u>tzi
at half past five	בחמש וחצי	be-<u>KHa</u>mesh va-<u>KHe</u>tzi
at seven o'clock	בשבע	be-<u>she</u>va
midday	שתים	<u>shtaym</u> es<u>reh</u>
	עשרה בצהריים	ba-<u>tzoho</u>rayim
midnight	חצות	<u>KHa</u>tzot

HOTELS

Israel's hotels are ranked by the Ministry of Tourism on a scale of 1 to 5 stars and the tourist and business traveller will have little difficulty in finding suitable accommodation. High-quality hotels are located in all the large cities such as Tel Aviv, Jerusalem, Haifa and Eilat. It is, however, vital to make reservations well in advance during the holiday seasons (Rosh Hashana, Christmas, Easter and Passover – see Cross-Cultural Notes p 10). Seaside resorts such as Eilat, Netanya and Nahariya have a wide variety of less expensive accommodation close to the beaches and often cater to tour groups. There is a good range of youth hostels located throughout the country and kibbutz guesthouses **bayt ha'araKHa** (בית האּרחה) can make an interesting alternative to hotels. Kibbutzim, communal agricultural settlements, are unique to Israel and a visit to one is a must on any tour of the country.

Christian hostels, situated primarily in the eastern section of Jerusalem, are similar to youth hostels but welcome all travellers. Most hotels in the Jewish areas of Israel keep kosher (the dietary laws prescribed in Judaism – see Cross-Cultural Notes p 9) and observe the Sabbath. For the tourist this will mean that Friday night and Saturday meals must be reserved in advance and that banking facilities, shops and other services will not be available until sunset on Saturday night. Prices are normally advertised in each hotel or are available from tourist information centres.

USEFUL WORDS AND PHRASES

balcony	מירפסת	mirpeset
bathroom	חדר אמבטיה	KHadar ambatia
bed	מיטה	mita
bedroom	חדר שינה	KHadar shayna
bill	חשבון	KHeshbon
breakfast	ארוחת בוקר	aruKHat boker
dining room	חדר אוכל	KHadar oKHel

23

dinner	ארוחת ערב	aruKHat erev
double room	חדר זוגי	KHeder zugi
foyer	לובי	lobi
full board	פנסיון מלא	pension maleh
half board	חצי פנסיון	KHatzi pension
hostel	אכסניה	aKHsaniya
hotel	מלון	malon
key	מפתח	mafteaKH
kibbutz guesthouse	בית הארחה	bayt ha'araKHa
lift	מעלית	ma'alit
lounge	אולם	ulam
lunch	ארוחת צהריים	aruKHat tzohorayim
manager	מנהל	menahel (m)
	מנהלת	menahelet (f)
reception	קבלה	kabala
receptionist	פקיד קבלה	pkid kabala (m)
	פקידת קבלה	pkidat kabala (f)
restaurant	מסעדה	mis'ada
room	חדר	KHeder
room service	שירות חדרים	sherut KHadarim
shower	מיקלחת	miklaKHat
single room	חדר ליחיד	KHeder le-yaKHid
toilet	שירותים	sherutim
twin room	חדר זוגי עם	KHeder zugi im mitot
	מיטות נפרדות	nifradot

Have you any vacancies?
יש לכם חדרים פנויים?
yesh laKHem KHadarim pnuyim?

I have a reservation
יש לי הזמנה לחדר
yesh li hazmana le-KHeder

I'd like a single/double room
אבקש חדר ליחיד/זוגי
ava<u>kesh</u> <u>KH</u>eder le-ya<u>KH</u>id/zugi

I'd like a twin room
אבקש חדר זוגי עם מיטות נפרדות
ava<u>kesh</u> <u>KH</u>eder zugi im mi<u>tot</u> nifra<u>dot</u>

I'd like a room with a bathroom/balcony
אבקש חדר עם אמבטיה/מירפסת
ava<u>kesh</u> <u>KH</u>eder im am<u>bat</u>ia/mir<u>pes</u>et

I'd like a room for one night/three nights
אבקש חדר ללילה אחד/לשלושה לילות
ava<u>kesh</u> <u>KH</u>eder le-<u>lai</u>la e<u>KH</u>ad/lish<u>lo</u>sha lay<u>lot</u>

What is the charge per night?
מה המחיר ללילה?
ma ha-me<u>KH</u>ir le-<u>lai</u>la?

I don't know yet how long I'll stay
עוד לא ידוע לי כמה זמן אשאר
od <u>l</u>o yadu'a li <u>ka</u>ma zman esha'<u>er</u>

When is breakfast/dinner?
מתי ארוחת הבוקר/הערב?
ma<u>tai</u> aru<u>KH</u>at ha-<u>bo</u>ker/ha-'<u>er</u>ev?

Would you have my luggage brought up?
אפשר בבקשה להעלות את המיזוודות שלי?
ef<u>shar</u> bevaka<u>sha</u> leha'a<u>lot</u> et ha-mizva<u>dot</u> she<u>li</u>?

Please call me at … o'clock
בבקשה לצלצל אלי בשעה ...
bevaka<u>sha</u> letzal<u>tzel</u> e<u>lai</u> besha'<u>a</u> ...

Can I have breakfast in my room?
אפשר לקבל ארוחת בוקר לחדר?
efshar lekabel aruKHat boker laKHeder?

I'll be back at ... o'clock
אחזור בשעה ...
eKHezor besha'a ...

My room number is ...
מספר החדר שלי הוא ...
mispar haKHeder sheli hu ...

I'm leaving tomorrow
אני עוזב/עוזבת מחר
ani ozev *(m)*/ozevet *(f)* maKHar

THINGS YOU'LL SEE

מים עמוקים	**mayim amukim**	deep water
חדר אוכל	**KHadar oKHel**	dining room
יציאת חירום	**yetzi'at KHerum**	emergency exit
כניסה	**knisa**	entrance
יציאה	**yetzi'a**	exit
גברים	**gvarim**	gents
נשים	**nashim**	ladies
ארוחת צהריים	**aruKHat tzohorayim**	lunch
הנהלה	**hanhala**	management
מנהל	**menahel**	manager
תפריט	**tafrit**	menu
אין כניסה	**ayn knisa**	no entry
אין יציאה	**ayn yetzi'a**	no exit
נא לנקות את החדר	**na lenakot et ha-KHeder**	please clean the room

→

נא לא להפריע	**na lo lehafri'a**	please do not disturb
נא לא לעשן	**na lo le'ashen**	please do not smoke
קבלה	**kabala**	reception
מים רדודים	**mayim redudim**	shallow water
חדר טלוויזיה	**KHadar televizia**	television room
שירותים	**sherutim**	toilets
לבריכת השחייה	**le-brayKHat ha-sKHiya**	to the swimming pool

THINGS YOU'LL HEAR

sliKHa, anaKHnu mele'im
I'm sorry, we're full

lo nish'aru KHadarim le-yaKHid/zugiyim
There are no single/double rooms left

le-kama laylot?
For how many nights?

ma shimKHa *(to a man)*/**ma shmeKH** *(to a woman)*?
What is your name?

eKH ata meshalem *(to a man)*/**eKH at meshalemet** *(to a woman)*?
How will you be paying?

bevakasha leshalem me-rosh
Please pay in advance

efshar lir'ot et ha-darkon bevakasha?
Can I see your passport please?

CAMPING

Israel offers much in the way of outdoor activities such as hiking and camping. There's a nationwide system of nature reserves and marked paths, as well as serviced campsites. Before setting out, however, it is imperative to check with a local tourist office or with the nature preservation authorities about camping permission, security regulations and weather conditions.

Due to the country's small size and closed borders, mobile caravans are not a practical way of travelling. Israel has an extensive network of good youth hostels, some of which are affiliated with the YHA, while others are private. Advance booking is recommended during the holiday periods and summer months.

Hitch-hiking is a common practice, but not a safe one. Lone men and women, and even two women together, are strongly advised not to hitch-hike, and to use the extensive bus service instead.

USEFUL WORDS AND PHRASES

campfire	מדורה	medura
campsite	(אתר) קמפינג	(atar) kemping
cooking utensils	כלי בישול	klay bishul
drinking water	מי שתיה	may shtiya
dustbin	פח אשפה	paKH ashpa
hitch-hike	לקחת טרמפים	lakaKHat trempim
hitch-hiking	טרמפ	tremp
kitchen	מטבח	mitbaKH
rope	חבל	KHevel
rubbish	אשפה	ashpa
rucksack	תרמיל גב	tarmil gav
saucepans	סירים	sirim
showers	מקלחות	miklaKHot
sink	כיור	kiyor
sleeping bag	שק שינה	sak shayna
tap	ברז	berez

28

tent	אוהל	<u>o</u>hel
toilets	שירותים	shayrut<u>im</u>
tourist office	מידע, מודיעין	may<u>da</u>, modi'<u>in</u>
youth hostel	אכסניית נוער	aKHsany<u>at</u> <u>no</u>'ar

Can I camp here?
אפשר להקים כאן אוהל?
ef<u>shar</u> lehak<u>im</u> kan <u>o</u>hel?

Where is the nearest campsite?
איפה יש בסביבה אתר קמפינג?
<u>ay</u>fo yesh ba-sv<u>iva</u> a<u>tar</u> <u>kemping</u>?

What is the charge per night?
כמה זה עולה ללילה?
<u>kama</u> zeh <u>oleh</u> le-<u>laila</u>?

Can I light a fire here?
אפשר להדליק כאן מדורה?
ef<u>shar</u> lehadl<u>ik</u> kan medu<u>ra</u>?

Where can I get ...?
איפה אפשר להשיג ...?
<u>ay</u>fo ef<u>shar</u> lehas<u>ig</u> ...?

Is there drinking water here?
יש כאן מי שתיה?
yesh kan may shti<u>ya</u>?

THINGS YOU'LL SEE OR HEAR

קמפינג	**<u>kemping</u>**	campsite
תשלום, תעריף	**tash<u>lum</u>, ta'<u>arif</u>**	charges

Hebrew	Transliteration	English
שטח סגור	shetaKH sagur	closed area
זהירות!	zehirut!	danger!
מי שתיה	may shtiya	drinking water
אש	esh	fire
שביל	shvil	footpath
להשכרה	lehaskara	for hire
מטבח	mitbaKH	kitchen
להשאיל	lehash'il	to lend
אור	or	light
תעודת חבר	te'udat KHaver	membership card
שטח צבאי	shetaKH tzva'i	military area
שמורת טבע	shmurat teva	nature reserve
לא להדליק אש	lo lehadlik esh	no campfires
אין כניסה	ayn knisa	no entry
מקלחת	miklaKHat	shower
שירותים	shayrutim	toilets
אכסניית נוער	aKHsanyat no'ar	youth hostel

MOTORING

In Israel you drive on the right and overtake on the left. There are several motorways, the main ones being Tel Aviv-Jerusalem and Tel Aviv-Haifa. There are no roundabouts. All secondary roads give way to main roads at junctions and crossroads, but in the case of roads or junctions being unmarked, the traffic coming from the RIGHT has priority.

The overall quality of roads is adequate, although smaller roads are often bumpy and have dangerous bends. Parking is a problem in Tel Aviv and you'll see many cars parked on pavements. Rush hour in the large cities is approximately between 7.30-9.00 a.m. The evening rush hour varies but tends to peak at around 5 p.m. Routes to Tel Aviv may become very busy on Saturday evenings too.

Distances and speed are always measured in kilometres. The speed limit on motorways is 90 km/h (55 mph), on other inter-city roads 80 km/h (50 mph), and in built-up areas 50 km/h (30 mph). Seat belts must be worn in the front seats at all times; seat belts in the back are compulsory for children up to the age of four.

Many petrol stations are open 24 hours a day. Fuel ratings are as follows: 91 octane/2-star **oktan tish'im ve-'aKHat** (91 אוקטן), 96 octane/4-star **oktan tish'im ve-shesh** (96 אוקטן) and diesel **dizel** (דיזל). Unleaded petrol **netul oferet** (נטול עופרת) has recently been introduced.

Israeli drivers can be aggressive and are seldom courteous; accident rates are, unfortunately, high. Be on the lookout for dangerous drivers, and don't take your right of way for granted!

SOME COMMON ROAD SIGNS

חניון	**KHenyon**	car park
זהירות	**zehirut**	caution

→

ילדים חוצים את הכביש	yeladim KHotzim et ha-kvish	children crossing
הצטלבות	hitztalvut	crossroads
סכנה	sakana	danger
עקומה חדה	akuma KHada	dangerous bend
צומת מסוכן	tzomet mesukan	dangerous junction
עזרה ראשונה	ezra rishona	first aid
רכב כבד	reKHev kaved	for heavy vehicles
מוסך	musaKH	garage
תן זכות קדימה	ten zKHut kdima	give way
כבה אורות	kabeh orot	headlights off
הדלק אורות	hadlek orot	headlights on
צומת	tzomet	junction
איזור אש	ezor esh	military training area
כביש מהיר	kvish mahir	motorway
גשר צר	gesher tzar	narrow bridge
כביש צר	kvish tzar	narrow road
אין כניסה	ayn knisa	no entry
אין עקיפה	ayn akifa	no overtaking
אין חניה	ayn KHanaya	no parking
כביש חד סטרי	kvish KHad sitri	one-way street
חניה	KHanaya	parking
מעבר חציה	ma'avar khatziya	pedestrian crossing
מדרחוב	midreKHov	pedestrian precinct
הולכי רגל	holKHay regel	pedestrians
דלק	delek	petrol
תחנת דלק	taKHanat delek	petrol station
עבודות בכביש	avodot ba-kvish	roadworks
בית ספר	bayt sefer	school
רוח צד	ruaKH tzad	side wind
האט	ha'et	slow
עצור	atzor	stop
מעבר תת קרקעי	ma'avar tat karka'i	subway
מרכז העיר	merkaz ha-'ir	town centre

USEFUL WORDS AND PHRASES

automatic *(noun)*	אוטומטי	otomati
boot	תא מיטען	ta mit'an
brake *(noun)*	מעצור	ma'atzor
breakdown	תקלה	takala
car	מכונית	meKHonit
caravan	קרוון	karavan
clutch	קלץ'	klach
crossroads	הצטלבות	hitztalvut
to drive	לנהוג	linhog
engine	מנוע	mano'a
exhaust	אגזוז	egzoz
fanbelt	רצועת מאוורר	retzu'at me'avrer
garage *(for repairs)*	מוסך	musaKH
(for petrol)	תחנת דלק	taKHanat delek
gear	מהלך, הילוך	mahalaKH, hiluKH
headlights	אורות קדמיים	orot kidmiyim
junction *(on motorway)*	צומת, מחלף	tzomet, meKHlaf
kilometre	קילומטר	kilometer
licence	רשיון	rishayon
lorry	משאית	masa'it
manual gears	תיבת הילוכים ידנית	tayvat hiluKHim yadanit
mirror	ראי	re'i
motorbike	אופנוע	ofano'a
motorway	כביש מהיר	kvish mahir
number plate	לוחית זיהוי	luKHit zihui
petrol	דלק	delek
rear lights	אורות אחוריים	orot aKHoriyim
road	כביש	kvish
spares	חלקי חילוף	KHelkay KHiluf
speed *(noun)*	מהירות	mehirut
speed limit	מהירות מותרת	mehirut muteret
speedometer	ספידומטר	spidometer
steering wheel	הגה	hegeh

street	רחוב	reKHov
to tow	לגרור	ligror
traffic lights	רמזור	ramzor
tyre	צמיג	tzamig
van	רכב מסחרי	reKHev misKHari
wheel	גלגל	galgal
windscreen	שימשה קידמית	shimsha kidmit
windscreen wiper	וישר	visher

I'd like some petrol/oil/water
דלק/שמן/מים, בבקשה
delek/shemen/mayim, bevakasha

Fill her up please!
מלא, בבקשה!
maleh, bevakasha!

I'd like 10 litres of petrol
עשרה ליטר דלק, בבקשה
asara liter delek, bevakasha

Would you check the tyres please?
אפשר לבדוק את הצמיגים, בבקשה?
efshar livdok et ha-tzmigim, bevakasha?

Do you do repairs?
אתם עושים תיקונים?
atem osim tikunim?

Can you repair the clutch?
אפשר לתקן את הקליץ'?
efshar letaken et ha-klach?

How long will it take?
כמה זמן זה יקח?
kama zman zeh yikaKH?

34

Where can I park?
איפה אפשר לחנות?
<u>ay</u>fo ef<u>shar</u> laKH<u>not</u>?

There is something wrong with the engine
יש בעייה במנוע
yesh be<u>'ay</u>a ba-ma<u>no</u>'a

The engine is overheating
המנוע מתחמם
ha-ma<u>no</u>'a mitKHa<u>mem</u>

I need a new tyre
צריך צמיג חדש
tariKH tza<u>mig</u> KHa<u>dash</u>

I'd like to hire a car
אבקש לשכור מכונית
ava<u>kesh</u> lis<u>kor</u> meKHo<u>nit</u>

Is there a mileage charge?
יש חיוב נוסף לפי קילומטרים?
yesh KHi<u>yuv</u> no<u>saf</u> le<u>fi</u> kilo<u>me</u>trim?

Where is the nearest garage?
איפה המוסך הקרוב ביותר?
<u>ay</u>fo ha-mu<u>saKH</u> ha-ka<u>rov</u> bayo<u>ter</u>?

How do I get to ...?
איך מגיעים ל...?
ayKH magi<u>'im</u> le-...?

Is this the road to ...?
זאת הדרך ל...?
zot ha-<u>dere</u>KH le-...?

35

DIRECTIONS YOU MAY BE GIVEN

yashar	straight on
mismol	on the left
smola	turn left
miyamin	on the right
yamina	turn right
rishon miyamin	first on the right
sheni mismol	second on the left
aKHaray ha-...	past the ...

THINGS YOU'LL SEE

לחץ אוויר	**laKHatz avir**	air pressure
נתיב איטי	**nativ iti**	crawler lane
דיזל	**dizel**	diesel
יציאה	**yetzi'a**	exit
אוקטן 96	**oktan tish'im ve-shesh**	4-star
כביש מהיר	**kvish mahir**	motorway
צומת, מחלף	**tzomet, meKHlaf**	motorway junction
שמן	**shemen**	oil
גובה שמן	**gova shemen**	oil level
דלק	**delek**	petrol
תחנת דלק	**taKHanat delek**	petrol station
תיקון	**tikun**	repair
פקק תנועה	**pkak tnu'a**	traffic jam
אוקטן 91	**oktan tish'im ve-aKHat**	2-star
לחץ צמיגים	**laKHatz tzmigim**	tyre pressure
נטול עופרת	**netul oferet**	unleaded

36

THINGS YOU'LL HEAR

otomati o yadani?
Would you like an automatic or a manual?

rishayon, bevakasha
May I see your licence?

RAIL TRAVEL

Israel's rail network is limited and far surpassed by the efficient bus system (see BY BUS AND TAXI p 48). Most trains are old, facilities simple, and distances relatively short. The best service runs from Tel Aviv to Haifa, via Netanya; it is regular and fast enough to offer a real alternative to road travel. The train ride from Tel Aviv up to Jerusalem is slow, but it is well worth making as a leisure trip for the beautiful scenery. A new urban railway system is currently being planned for Tel Aviv and its metropolitan area.

USEFUL WORDS AND PHRASES

booking office	משרד כרטיסים	misrad kartisim
buffet	מזנון	miznon
carriage	קרון	karon
engine	קטר	katar
entrance	כניסה	knisa
exit	יציאה	yetzi'a
first class	מחלקה ראשונה	maKHlaka rishona
to get in	להיכנס	lehikanes
to get out	לצאת	latzet
left luggage office	שמירת חפצים	shmirat KHafatzim
lost property office	אבידות	avaydot
luggage trolley	עגלת מיטען	eglat mit'an
platform	רציף	ratzif
railway	מסילת ברזל	mesilat barzel
reserved seat	מקום שמור	makom shamur
restaurant car	קרון מסעדה	kron mis'ada
return ticket	כרטיס הלוך ושוב	kartis haloKH vashov
seat	מושב	moshav
second class	מחלקה שניה	maKHlaka shniya
single ticket	כרטיס בכיוון אחד	kartis beKHivun eKHad
station	תחנה	taKHana
ticket	כרטיס	kartis

ticket collector	מבקר כרטיסים	mevaker kartisim
timetable	לוח זמנים	luaKH zmanim
train	רכבת	rakevet
waiting room	חדר המתנה	KHadar hamtana
window	חלון	KHalon

When does the train for ... leave?
מתי הרכבת ל...?
matai ha-rakevet le-...?

When is the next train to ...?
מתי הרכבת הבאה ל...?
matai ha-rakevet ha-ba'a le-...?

When is the first train to ...?
מתי הרכבת הראשונה ל...?
matai ha-rakevet ha-rishona le-...?

When is the last train to ...?
מתי הרכבת האחרונה ל...?
matai ha-rakevet ha-aKHrona le-...?

What is the fare to ...?
כמה עולה כרטיס ל...?
kama oleh kartis le-...?

Does the train stop at ...?
הרכבת עוצרת ב...?
ha-rakevet otzeret be-...?

How long does it take to get to ...?
כמה זמן הנסיעה ל...?
kama zman ha-nesi'a le-...?

A single/return ticket to ... please
כרטיס בכיוון אחד/הלוך ושוב ל..., בבקשה
kartis beKHivun eKHad/haloKH va-shov le-..., bevakasha

39

I'd like to reserve a seat
אבקש מקום שמור
avakesh makom shamur

Is this the right train for ...?
זו הרכבת ל...?
zo ha-rakevet le-...?

Is the train late?
הרכבת מאחרת?
ha-rakevet me'aKHeret?

Could you help me with my luggage please?
אפשר לקבל עזרה עם המיטען, בבקשה?
efshar lekabel ezra im ha-mit'an, bevakasha?

Is this a non-smoking compartment?
זה קרון ללא מעשנים?
zeh karon lelo me'ashnim?

Is this seat free?
המושב הזה פנוי?
ha-moshav ha-zeh panui?

This seat is taken
המושב הזה תפוס
ha-moshav ha-zeh tafus

I have reserved this seat
המושב הזה שמור לי
ha-moshav ha-zeh shamur li

May I open/close the window?
אפשר לפתוח/לסגור את החלון?
efshar lifto'aKH/lisgor et ha-KHalon?

What station is this?
איזו תחנה זאת?
ayzo taKHana zot?

Do we stop at …?
עוצרים ב...?
otzrim be-...?

Would you keep an eye on my things for a moment?
תוכל/תוכלי בבקשה לשים עין על הדברים שלי לרגע?
tuKHal *(to a man)*/tuKHli *(to a woman)* bevakasha lasim ayin
al ha-dvarim sheli le-rega?

THINGS YOU'LL SEE

מזנון	**miznon**	buffet
קרון	**karon**	carriage
עיכוב	**ikuv**	delay
מעצור חירום	**ma'atzor KHerum**	emergency brake
תפוס	**tafus**	engaged
כניסה	**knisa**	entrance
יציאה	**yetzi'a**	exit
מידע, מודיעין	**mayda, modi'in**	information
שמירת חפצים	**shmirat KHafatzim**	left luggage
אין כניסה	**ayn knisa**	no entry
לא מעשנים	**lo me'ashnim**	no smoking
רציף	**ratzif**	platform
מעשנים	**me'ashnim**	smokers
קופה	**kupa**	ticket office
כרטיסים	**kartisim**	tickets
לוח זמנים	**luaKH zmanim**	timetable
חדר המתנה	**KHadar hamtana**	waiting room

41

THINGS YOU'LL HEAR

zehir<u>ut</u>
Attention, be careful

kartis<u>im</u>, bevaka<u>sha</u>
Tickets please

AIR TRAVEL

Israel's main international airport is the Ben-Gurion Airport, fifteen minutes drive to Tel Aviv and forty minutes to Jerusalem. Some international flights land in Eilat, and the domestic connections include smaller airports in northern Tel Aviv, Jerusalem, and the north of the country. However, Israel's size means that all destinations are within easy driving distance. Travellers planning to go to Arab countries, with the exception of Egypt, may do well to request that their passport is not stamped by the Israeli passport control.

USEFUL WORDS AND PHRASES

aircraft	מטוס	matos
air hostess	דיילת	dayelet
airline	חברת תעופה	KHevrat te'ufa
airport	שדה תעופה	sdeh te'ufa
airport bus	אוטובוס שדה תעופה	otobus sdeh te'ufa
aisle seat	מושב ליד המעבר	moshav leyad ha-ma'avar
arrivals	טיסות נכנסות	tisot niKHnasot
baggage (claim)	מיטען	mit'an
boarding card	כרטיס עליה למטוס	kartis aliya la-matos
check-in	צ'ק אין	chek in
check-in desk	דלפק קבלת נוסעים	dalpak kabalat nos'im
customs	מכס	meKHes
delay	עיכוב	ikuv
departure	טיסות יוצאות	tisot yotz'ot
departure lounge	אולם נוסעים יוצאים	ulam nos'im yotz'im
emergency exit	יציאת חירום	yetzi'at KHerum
flight	טיסה	tisa
flight number	מיספר טיסה	mispar tisa
gate	שער	sha'ar

43

jet	סילון	silon
land *(verb)*	לנחות	linKHot
long distance flight	טיסה ארוכה	tisa aruka
passport	דרכון	darkon
passport control	ביקורת דרכונים	bikoret darkonim
pilot	טייס	tayas
runway	מסלול	maslul
seat	מושב	moshav
seat belt	חגורת בטיחות	KHagorat betiKHut
steward	דייל	dayal
stewardess	דיילת	dayelet
take-off	המראה	hamra'a
window	חלון	KHalon
wing	כנף	kanaf

When is there a flight to ...?
מתי יש טיסה ל...?
matai yesh tisa le-...?

What time does the flight to ... leave?
מתי יוצאת הטיסה ל...?
matai yotzet ha-tisa le-...?

Is it a direct flight?
זאת טיסה ישירה?
zot tisa yeshira?

Do I have to change planes?
צריך להחליף מטוס?
tzariKH lehaKHlif matos?

When do I have to check in?
מתי צריך להגיע לטיסה?
matai tzariKH lehagi'a la-tisa?

I'd like a single ticket to ...
אבקש כרטיס טיסה בכיוון אחד ל...
avakesh kartis tisa be-KHivun eKHad le-...

I'd like a return ticket to ...
אבקש כרטיס טיסה הלוך ושוב ל...
avakesh kartis tisa haloKH va-shov le-...

I'd like a non-smoking seat please
לא מעשנים, בבקשה
lo me'ashnim, bevakasha

I'd like a window seat please
ליד החלון, בבקשה
leyad ha-KHalon, bevakasha

How long will the flight be delayed?
כמה זמן הטיסה מתעכבת?
kama zman ha-tisa mit'akevet?

Is this the right gate for the ... flight?
זה השער הנכון לטיסה ל...?
zeh ha-sha'ar ha-naKHon la-tisa le-...?

Which gate for the flight to ...?
איזה שער לטיסה ל...?
ayzeh sha'ar la-tisa le-...?

When do we arrive in ...?
מתי נגיע ל...?
matai nagi'a le-...?

May I smoke now?
אפשר לעשן עכשיו?
efshar le'ashen aKHshav?

I do not feel very well

אני לא מרגיש/מרגישה טוב

a<u>ni</u> lo mar<u>gish</u> *(m)*/margi<u>sha</u> *(f)* tov

Please don't stamp my passport

בבקשה לא להחתים את הדרכון שלי

bevaka<u>sha</u> lo lehaKH<u>tim</u> et ha-dar<u>kon</u> she<u>li</u>

THINGS YOU'LL SEE

מטוס	**ma<u>tos</u>**	aircraft
גובה	**go<u>va</u>**	altitude
טיסות נכנסות	**ti<u>sot</u> niKH<u>nasot</u>**	arrivals
מיטען	**mit'<u>an</u>**	baggage (claim)
טיסת צ'ארטר	**ti<u>sat</u> charter**	charter flight
ביקורת מכס	**bi<u>koret</u> meKH<u>es</u>**	customs control
עיכוב	**i<u>kuv</u>**	delay
טיסות יוצאות	**ti<u>sot</u> yotz'<u>ot</u>**	departures
טיסה ישירה	**ti<u>sa</u> yeshi<u>ra</u>**	direct flight
טיסת פנים	**ti<u>sat</u> pnim**	domestic flight
יציאת חירום	**yetzi'<u>at</u> KHe<u>rum</u>**	emergency exit
נחיתת חירום	**neKHi<u>tat</u> KHe<u>rum</u>**	emergency landing
נא להדק חגורות	**na leha<u>dek</u> KHago<u>rot</u>**	fasten seat belt
טיסה	**ti<u>sa</u>**	flight
שער	**sha'<u>ar</u>**	gate
מידע, מודיעין	**may<u>da</u>, modi'<u>in</u>**	information
נחיתת ביניים	**neKHi<u>tat</u> bay<u>nayim</u>**	intermediate stop
טיסה בינלאומית	**ti<u>sa</u> baynle'u<u>mit</u>**	international flight
נחיתה	**neKHi<u>ta</u>**	landing
זמן מקומי	**zman meko<u>mi</u>**	local time
לא מעשנים	**lo me'ash<u>nim</u>**	non-smokers
לא לעשן	**lo le'a<u>shen</u>**	no smoking please

→

נוסעים	**nos'im**	passengers
דרכון	**darkon**	passport
ביקורת דרכונים	**bikoret darkonim**	passport control
טיסה סדירה	**tisa sdira**	scheduled flight
דייל	**dayal**	steward
דיילת	**dayelet**	stewardess
המראה	**hamra'a**	take-off

THINGS YOU'LL HEAR

ha-nos'im be-tisa ... mitbakshim lageshet le-sha'ar ...
The flight for ... is now boarding at gate ...

zohi kri'a aKHrona le-tisa ...
This is the last call for flight ...

BY BUS AND TAXI

Bus travel is perhaps the least expensive and most efficient way to get around in Israel. Cities and towns are linked together by a regular, frequent and usually air-conditioned bus service which runs from dawn until midnight from Sunday to Thursday. Generally, buses stop running on Friday afternoons because of the Sabbath and services are resumed on Saturday night, although on Saturday a limited bus service now operates in Tel Aviv, Haifa and Eilat. Inter-city tickets are purchased at the bus station and while during the week there's usually no queue, on Friday afternoons and Sunday mornings you might find yourself amongst crowds of soldiers and civilians going to or returning from relatives. There are discounts on inter-city tickets for senior citizens, students and children. The bus services within the cities are also fast and efficient and you can purchase your ticket from the driver or conductor. There is a multiple-journey ticket, **kartisiya** (כרטיסיה), which can also be purchased from the driver and which can save you money if you're travelling around a lot. Discounts on these tickets are available for senior citizens and children. A monthly bus pass, **KHodshi KHofshi** (חודשי חופשי), allowing unlimited travel in Tel Aviv is also available.

Sometimes to avoid the jostling crowd the traveller may prefer to take a taxi. There are two types of taxi travel. One is just as in the West where it's possible to book a taxi by phone or flag one down in the street. Most have meters, but if they don't it is essential that you agree in advance on the fare. The other type of taxi, called the **sherut** (שירות), is available for travel between the larger cities such as Tel Aviv, Jerusalem, Haifa and Beer Sheba, and to and from the airport. These taxis are shared between about seven passengers and have a fixed route and price. The taxi and the **sherut** are also available for hire on Friday nights and Saturdays at a slightly increased fare. Tipping the taxi driver is not customary in Israel.

USEFUL WORDS AND PHRASES

adult	מבוגר	mevugar
bus	אוטובוס	otobus
bus map	מפת מסלולי אוטובוס	mapat maslulay otobus
bus stop	תחנת אוטובוס	taKHanat otobus
child	ילד	yeled
coach	אוטובוס	otobus
conductor	כרטיסן	kartisan
connection	קשר	kesher
driver	נהג/נהגת	nahag (m)/naheget (f)
fare	דמי נסיעה	dmay nesiya
main bus station	תחנה מרכזית	taKHana merkazit
monthly bus pass	חודשי חופשי	KHodshi KHofshi
multiple-journey ticket	כרטיסיה	kartisiya
number 5 bus	אוטובוס מספר חמש	otobus mispar KHamesh
passenger	נוסע/נוסעת	nose'a (m)/nosa'at (f)
seat	מושב	moshav
subway	מעבר תת קרקעי	ma'avar tat karka'i
taxi	מונית	monit
(fixed route)	שירות	sherut
terminus	תחנה סופית	taKHana sofit
ticket	כרטיס	kartis

Where is the main bus station?
איפה התחנה המרכזית?
ayfo ha-taKHana ha-merkazit?

Where is there a bus stop?
איפה יש תחנת אוטובוס?
ayfo yesh taKHanat otobus?

Which bus goes to ...?
איזה אוטובוס נוסע ל...?
ayzeh otobus nose'a le-...?

How often does the bus to ... run?
כל כמה זמן נוסע האוטובוס ל...?
kol <u>kama</u> zman no<u>se</u>'a ha-<u>o</u>tobus le-...?

Would you tell me when we get to ...?
אפשר להגיד לי מתי מגיעים ל...?
ef<u>shar</u> lehagid li ma<u>tai</u> magi<u>'im</u> le-...?

Do I have to get off yet?
אני צריך/צריכה לרדת?
a<u>ni</u> tzari<u>KH</u> (m)/tzri<u>KHa</u> (f) la<u>redet</u>?

How do you get to ...?
איך מגיעים ל...?
ay<u>KH</u> magi<u>'im</u> le-...?

Is it very far?
האם זה רחוק?
ha-<u>im</u> zeh ra<u>KHok</u>?

I want to go to ...
אני רוצה לנסוע ל.../אני רוצה לנסוע ל...
a<u>ni</u> rot<u>zeh</u> (m) lin<u>so</u>'a le-... /a<u>ni</u> rot<u>za</u> (f) lin<u>so</u>'a le-...

Do you go near ...?
אתה עובר על-יד...?
a<u>ta</u> <u>over</u> al-yad ...?

Where can I buy a ticket?
איפה אפשר לקנות כרטיס?
<u>ayfo</u> ef<u>shar</u> lik<u>not</u> kartis?

Could you open/close the window?
אפשר לפתוח/לסגור את החלון?
ef<u>shar</u> lifto<u>aKH</u>/lis<u>gor</u> et ha-KHa<u>lon</u>?

Could you help me get a ticket?
אפשר לעזור לי לקנות כרטיס?
efshar la'azor li liknot kartis?

Please don't push
בבקשה לא לדחוף
bevakasha lo lidKHof

When does the last bus leave?
מתי עוזב האוטובוס האחרון?
matai ozev ha-otobus ha-aKHaron?

To ... please
ל... בבקשה
le-... bevakasha

How much will it cost?
כמה זה יעלה?
kama zeh ya'aleh?

Can you wait here and take me back?
תוכל לחכות כאן ולהחזיר אותי?
tuKHal leKHakot kan ve-lehaKHzir oti?

THINGS YOU'LL SEE

מבוגרים	**mevugarim**	adults
מיזוג אוויר	**mizug avir**	air-conditioning
שים לב לחפץ	**sim lev le-KHefetz**	beware of
חשוד!	**KHashud**	suspicious objects
להחליף	**lehaKHlif**	to change
ילדים	**yeladim**	children
נסיעה	**nesi'a**	departure, journey

51

נא לא להפריע לנהג	na lo lehafri'a la-nahag	do not speak to the driver
יציאת חירום	yetzi'at KHerum	emergency exit
כניסה	knisa	entrance
כניסה מקדימה/ מאחור	knisa mi-kadima mi-aKHor	entry at the front/ rear
יציאה	yetzi'a	exit
מלא	maleh	full
כרטיסיה	kartisiya	multiple-journey ticket
אין כְּניסה	ayn knisa	no entry
נא לא לעשן	na lo le'ashen	no smoking
דרך	dereKH	road
מסלול	maslul	route
מושב	moshav	seat
עצור	atzor	stop
תחנת מוניות	taKHanat moniyot	taxi rank
תחנה סופית	taKHana sofit	terminus
כרטיס	kartis	ticket

RESTAURANTS

Israel offers a rich variety of gastronomic experiences. The Israeli cuisine is, typically, a blend of favourite dishes from the Middle East and from Europe; a more sophisticated cuisine, with the emphasis on fish and fruit, is also available. The Israeli breakfast is often a sumptuous meal, consisting of a fresh vegetable salad, eggs, and several types of cheese, cold meat or fish. Coffee is the most popular hot beverage. Lunch is the big hot meal of the day, while supper, especially in private homes, is usually smaller and often vegetarian.

Israel's restaurants are similar to those in the West as far as style and variety are concerned: everything from Mexican to Chinese can be found. In larger cities, the waiters are often students; service is friendly, although not always professional. There's usually an optional service charge of between 10-15%. Set menus are uncommon, and most restaurants offer only a choice of à la carte dishes. A reservation is needed for the popular or upmarket establishments, especially at the weekend. At the other end of the spectrum, nutritious and cheap food can be bought from street stands and kiosks; the most typical of such dishes is **falafel** (פלפל), fried chickpea balls served in pitta bread with ground chickpea sauce **кHumus** (חומום), salad and pickles.

Many, though by no means all, of Israel's restaurants keep kosher, the dietary laws (see Cross-Cultural Notes p 9), and will close on Friday nights and all day on Saturday. If you happen to be in Jerusalem or Galilee at this time, delicious Arab cuisine is to be recommended: ask for a **maza**, and you will be given a variety of small, tasty hors d'œuvres.

Alcoholic drinks are served in most restaurants and bars: Israel produces its own wine and lager-style beer, and imports European products. There is a good range of fruit drinks. Tap water is usually drinkable; mineral water, local and imported, is widely available.

USEFUL WORDS AND PHRASES

English	Hebrew	Transliteration
bar	באר	bar
beer	בירה	bira
bill	חשבון	KHeshbon
bottle	בקבוק	bakbuk
breakfast	ארוחת בוקר	aruKHat boker
café	בית קפה	bayt kafeh
cake	עוגה	uga
chef	טבח, טבחית	tabaKH (m), tabaKHit (f)
coffee	קפה	kafeh
cup	ספל	sefel
fork	מזלג	mazleg
glass	כום	kos
knife	סכין	sakin
lunch	ארוחת צהריים	aruKHat tzohorayim
meal	ארוחה	aruKHa
menu	תפריט	tafrit
milk	חלב	KHalav
plate	צלחת	tzalakhat
receipt	קבלה	kabala
sandwich	כריך, סנדוויץ'	kariKH, sendvich
serviette	מפית	mapit
snack (sandwich etc)	חטיף	KHatif
(a light meal)	ארוחה קלה	aruKHa kala
snack bar	מזנון	miznon
soup	מרק	marak
spoon	כף	kaf
sugar	סוכר	sukar
supper	ארוחת ערב	aruKHat erev
table	שולחן	shulKHan
tea	תה	teh
teaspoon	כפית	kapit
tip	תשר, טיפ	tip, tesher
vegetarian	צמחוני, צמחונית	tzimKHoni (m), tzimKHonit (f)
waiter	מלצר	meltzar

waitress	מלצרית	meltza<u>rit</u>
water	מים	mayim
wine	יין	yayin
wine list	תפריט יינות	tafrit yay<u>not</u>

A table for one please
שולחן ליחיד, בבקשה
shul<u>KH</u>an le-ya<u>KH</u>id, bevaka<u>sha</u>

A table for two please
שולחן לשניים, בבקשה
shul<u>KH</u>an le-<u>shnay</u>im, bevaka<u>sha</u>

Can I see the menu?
אפשר לראות את התפריט?
ef<u>shar</u> lir'<u>ot</u> et ha-taf<u>rit</u>?

Can I see the wine list?
אפשר לראות את תפריט היינות?
ef<u>shar</u> lir'<u>ot</u> et tafrit ha-yay<u>not</u>?

What would you recommend?
על מה אתה ממליץ?
al <u>ma</u> <u>ata</u> mamlitz? *(to a man)*
על מה את ממליצה?
al <u>ma</u> at mamlit<u>za</u>? *(to a woman)*

I'd like ...
אני מבקש/מבקשת ...
a<u>ni</u> meva<u>kesh</u> *(m)*/meva<u>keshet</u> *(f)* ...

Just a cup of coffee, please
רק כום קפה, בבקשה
rak kos ka<u>feh</u>, bevaka<u>sha</u>

RESTAURANTS

Excuse me!
סליחה!
sliKHa!

Can we have the bill, please?
אפשר לקבל את החשבון, בבקשה?
efshar lekabel et ha-KHeshbon, bevakasha?

I only want a snack
רק משהו קל, בבקשה
rak mashehu kal, bevakasha

I didn't order this
לא הזמנתי את זה
lo hizmanti et zeh

May we have some more ...?
אפשר לקבל עוד ...?
efshar lekabel od ...?

The meal was very good, thank you
זה היה טוב מאד, תודה רבה
zeh haya tov meod, toda raba

My compliments to the chef!
כל הכבוד לטבח!
kol hakavod la-tabaKH!

THINGS YOU'LL SEE

סגור	**sagur**	closed
קפה	**kafeh**	coffee house, café
פלפל	**falafel**	falafel
קיוסק	**kiyosk**	kiosk

→

56

כשר	**kasher**	kosher
פתוח	**patua**KH	open
מסעדה	**mis'ada**	restaurant
מזנון	**miznon**	snack bar

THINGS YOU'LL HEAR

anaKHnu mele'im
We are fully booked

be-te'avon!
Enjoy your meal!

ma tishtu?
What would you like to drink?

MENU READER

(* an asterisk indicates a dish which would not be served in a kosher restaurant)

STARTERS, SOUPS AND SALADS

מתאבן	**meta'aben**	appetizer
מרק עוף	**marak off**	chicken soup
כבד קצוץ	**kaved katzutz**	chopped liver
כופתאות	**kufta'ot**	dumplings, matzo balls
ביצה רוסית	**baytza rusit**	egg mayonnaise
פלאפל	**falafel**	falafel – fried chick pea balls in pitta bread with salad and hot pepper sauce
מנה ראשונה	**mana rishona**	first course
חומוס	**KHumus**	humous (chick peas or ground chick pea paste) served with pitta bread and salad
מרק עדשים	**marak adashim**	lentil soup
חמוצים	**KHamutzim**	pickles (cucumber, tomato, pepper etc)

סלט תפוחי אדמה	**sal<u>at</u> tapu<u>KH</u>ay ad<u>a</u>ma**	potato salad
סלט	**sal<u>at</u>**	salad
סלט חריף	**sal<u>at</u> <u>KH</u>ar<u>if</u>**	spicy salad, usually with hot peppers
חציל ממולא	**<u>KH</u>a<u>tzil</u> memu<u>la</u>**	stuffed aubergine
פלפל ממולא	**pil<u>pel</u> memu<u>la</u>**	stuffed pepper
שזיפים ממולאים	**shezi<u>fim</u> memula'<u>im</u>**	stuffed prunes
ממולאים	**memula'<u>im</u>**	stuffed vegetables or fruit
מרק	**ma<u>rak</u>**	soup
סלט ירקות	**sal<u>at</u> yera<u>kot</u>**	vegetable salad
מרק ירקות	**ma<u>rak</u> yera<u>kot</u>**	vegetable soup

EGGS, CHEESE AND PASTA

גבינה	**gvi<u>na</u>**	cheese
גבינת קוטג'	**gvi<u>nat</u> <u>kotej</u>**	cottage cheese
גבינת שמנת	**gvi<u>nat</u> sha<u>me</u>net**	cream cheese (high-fat)
גבינה לבנה	**gvi<u>na</u> le<u>va</u>na**	cream cheese (low- or medium-fat)
ביצה	**bay<u>tza</u>**	egg
ביצה קשה	**bay<u>tza</u> ka<u>sha</u>**	hard-boiled egg
גבינה קשה	**gvi<u>na</u> ka<u>sha</u>**	hard cheese
גבינה צהובה	**gvi<u>na</u> tze<u>hu</u>ba**	hard, yellow, mild cheese

59

אטריות	**itri<u>yot</u>**	noodles
חביתה	**KHavi<u>ta</u>**	omelette
פסטה	**<u>pasta</u>**	pasta
ביצה מקושקשת	**<u>baytza</u> mekush<u>ke</u>shet**	scrambled eggs
ביצה רכה	**<u>baytza ra</u>ka**	soft-boiled egg

FISH

קרפיון	**karpi<u>yon</u>**	carp
פילה	**fil<u>eh</u>**	fillet
דג	**dag**	fish
דג ממולא	**dag memu<u>la</u>**	gefilte fish – a seasoned fish ball
סלמון	**sal<u>mon</u>**	salmon
דג מלוח	**dag ma<u>lua</u>KH**	salted herring
פירות ים	**pay<u>rot</u> yam**	seafood*
חסילונים	**KHasilo<u>nim</u>**	shrimps, prawns*
סול	**sol**	sole
קלמרי	**kala<u>ma</u>ri**	squid*
אמנון	**am<u>nun</u>**	St Peter's fish (freshwater fish from Sea of Galilee)
פורל	**for<u>el</u>**	trout

MEAT, FOWL, OFFAL

בקר	**ba<u>kar</u>**	beef
מוח	**<u>moa</u>KH**	brains
חזה	**KHa<u>zeh</u>**	breast
עוף	**off**	chicken
ברווז	**bar<u>vaz</u>**	duck
פילה	**<u>fileh</u>**	fillet
גולש	**<u>gulash</u>**	goulash
טלה	**ta<u>leh</u>**	lamb
רגל	**<u>regel</u>**	leg
כבד	**ka<u>ved</u>**	liver
בשר	**ba<u>sar</u>**	meat
שיפוד	**shi<u>pud</u>**	meat on a skewer
כבש	**<u>keves</u>**	mutton, lamb
בשר לבן	**ba<u>sar</u> la<u>van</u>**	pork*
צלע	**<u>tzela</u>**	rib
נקניק	**nak<u>nik</u>**	sausage
שניצל	**sh<u>nitzel</u>**	schnitzel – slice of veal, coated in breadcrumbs and fried
אומצה, סטייק	**um<u>tza</u>, stayk**	steak
צלי	**tzli**	stew
לשון	**la<u>shon</u>**	tongue

61

תרנגול הודו	**tarnegol hodu**	turkey
עגל	**egel**	veal

MAIN DISHES

חמין	**KHamin**	cholent, a rich stew of meat, beans and potatoes
שקשוקה	**shakshuka**	dish of fried vegetables and egg
קבב	**kabab**	lamb kebab
מנה עיקרית	**mana ikarit**	main course
קציצה	**ketzitza**	meat balls, served with rice or vegetables
בורקם	**burekas**	pasties filled with cheese or potatoes
שווארמה	**shawarma**	pieces of roasted lamb
סטייק לבן	**stayk lavan**	pork steak*
ששליק	**shishlik**	shish kebab – pieces of meat and vegetables grilled on a skewer
אומצה, סטייק	**umtza, stayk**	steak

| בלינצ׳ם | __blinches__ | thin pancakes filled with cheese or spinach |

VEGETABLES

ארטישוק	__artishok__	artichoke
חציל	__KHatzil__	aubergine
אבוקדו	__avokado__	avocado
שעועית	__she'u'it__	beans
כרוב	__kruv__	cabbage
גזר	__gezer__	carrot
כרובית	__kruvit__	cauliflower
צ׳יפם	__chips__	chips, French fries
קישוא	__kishu__	courgette
מלפפון	__melafefon__	cucumber
תפוחי אדמה מטוגנים	__tapuKHay adama metuganim__	fried potatoes
שום	__shum__	garlic
פלפל ירוק	__pilpel yarok__	green pepper
עדשים	__adashim__	lentils
חסה	__KHasa__	lettuce
פטריות	__pitriyot__	mushrooms
זיתים	__zaytim__	olives
בצל	__batzal__	onion
אפונה	__afuna__	peas

פלפל	**pilpel**	pepper
תפוח אדמה	**tapuaKH adama**	potato
עגבניה	**agvanya**	tomato
תרד	**tered**	spinach
בצל ירוק	**batzal yarok**	spring onion
תירס	**tiras**	sweetcorn
ירקות	**yerakot**	vegetables
סלט ירקות	**salat yerakot**	vegetable salad
ירקות העונה	**yerakot ha-'ona**	vegetables of the season

FRUIT, NUTS AND SEEDS

שקדים	**shkedim**	almonds
תפוח עץ	**tapuaKH etz**	apple
משמש	**mishmesh**	apricot
בננה	**banana**	banana
תמר	**tamar**	date
תאנה	**te'ena**	fig
פירות	**payrot**	fruit
פרי	**pri**	fruit
פירות העונה	**payrot ha-'ona**	fruit of the season
ענבים	**anavim**	grapes
אשכולית	**eshkolit**	grapefruit
לימון	**limon**	lemon

מנגו	**mango**	mango
מלון	**melon**	melon
אגוזים	**egozim**	nuts, walnuts
תפוז	**tapuz**	orange
אפרסק	**afarsek**	peach
בוטנים	**botnim**	peanuts
אגס	**agas**	pear
אננס	**ananas**	pineapple
פיסטוק חלבי	**fistuk KHalabi**	pistachio nuts
שזיף	**shezif**	plum
רימון	**rimon**	pomegranate
תות שדה	**tut sadeh**	strawberry
גרעינים	**gar'inim**	sunflower seeds
אבטיח	**avatiaKH**	watermelon

CAKES AND DESSERTS

עוגיה	**ugiya**	biscuit
עוגה	**uga**	cake
עוגת גבינה	**ugat gvina**	cheesecake
עוגת שוקולד	**ugat shokolad**	chocolate cake
מוס שוקולד	**mus shokolad**	chocolate mousse
קרם קרמל	**krem karamel**	crème caramel
קרם בוריה	**krem bavaria**	custard-like dessert made from eggs and vanilla

מנה אחרונה	**ma<u>na</u> aKHaro<u>na</u>**	dessert
קינוח	**kinuaKH**	dessert
סופגנייה	**sufganya**	doughnut
סלט פירות	**sa<u>lat</u> pay<u>rot</u>**	fruit salad
טורט	**tort**	gâteau
גלידה	**<u>gli</u>da**	ice cream
מוס	**mus**	mousse
בלינצ׳ים	**<u>blin</u>ches**	thin pancakes filled with chocolate or sweet cheese
עוגת שמרים	**u<u>gat</u> shma<u>rim</u>**	yeast cake

DRINKS

משקה חריף	**mash<u>keh</u> KHa<u>rif</u>**	alcoholic drink
בירה	**<u>bi</u>ra**	beer
קפה שחור	**ka<u>feh</u> shaKHor**	black coffee
בירה בבקבוק	**<u>bi</u>ra be-bak<u>buk</u>**	bottled beer
לבן	**<u>le</u>ben**	buttermilk
בירה בפחית	**<u>bi</u>ra be-paKHit**	canned beer
שמפנייה	**sham<u>pan</u>ya**	champagne
שוקו קר	**<u>sho</u>ko kar**	cold chocolate
שוקו חם	**<u>sho</u>ko KHam**	hot chocolate
קקאו	**ka<u>ka</u>ʻo**	cocoa
קפה	**ka<u>feh</u>**	coffee

קפה נטול קפאין	**kafeh netul kafe'in**	decaffeinated coffee
בירה מהחבית	**bira me-ha-KHavit**	draught beer
משקה	**mashkeh**	drink
משקה תוסס	**mashkeh toses**	fizzy drink
תה צמחים	**teh tzmaKHim**	herbal tea
נס קפה	**nes kafeh**	instant coffee
מיץ	**mitz**	juice
לימונדה	**limonada**	lemonade
חלב	**KHalav**	milk
מילקשייק	**milkshayk**	milk shake
מים מינרליים	**mayim mineraliyim**	mineral water
מיץ תפוזים	**mitz tapuzim**	orange juice
יין אדום	**yayin adom**	red wine
סודה	**soda**	soda water
משקה קל	**mashkeh kal**	soft drink
יין נתזים	**yayn netazim**	sparkling wine
קפה בוץ	**kafeh botz**	strong black coffee
תה	**teh**	tea
תה עם לימון	**teh im limon**	tea with lemon
תה עם חלב	**teh im KHalav**	tea with milk
קפה תורכי/טורקי	**kafeh turki**	Turkish coffee
מים	**mayim**	water

קפה הפוך	**kafeh hafuKH**	white coffee
ין לבן	**yayin lavan**	white wine
ין	**yayin**	wine

BASIC FOODS

חמאה	**KHem'a**	butter
שמנת מתוקה	**shamenet metuka**	cream
דבש	**dvash**	honey
ריבה	**riba**	jam, marmalade
מרגרינה	**margarina**	margarine
מיונז	**mayonez**	mayonnaise
חרדל	**KHardal**	mustard
שמן	**shemen**	oil
שמן זית	**shemen zayit**	olive oil
ריבת תפוזים	**ribat tapuzim**	orange marmalade
אורז	**orez**	rice
רוטב	**rotev**	sauce, gravy
שמנת	**shamenet**	soured cream
חומץ	**KHometz**	vinegar
קצפת	**katzefet**	whipped cream
יונורט	**yogurt**	yoghurt

HERBS AND SPICES

זעתר	**za'atar**	herb similar to rosemary
פלפל חריף	**pilpel KHarif**	hot pepper or chilli powder
נענע	**na'ana**	mint
פלפל	**pilpel**	pepper
מלח	**melaKH**	salt
תבלין	**tavlin**	spice, herb

TYPES OF BREAD etc

לחם שחור	**leKHem shaKHor**	'black' (brown or wholemeal) bread
לחם	**leKHem**	bread
לחמניה	**laKHmanya**	bun, roll
חלה	**KHala**	challa – a rich, white Sabbath bread
מצה	**matza**	matzo – a crisp, unleavened Passover bread
פיתה	**pita**	pitta bread
לחם חי	**leKHem KHai**	wheatgerm bread
לחם לבן	**leKHem lavan**	white bread

MENU READER

SNACKS

פלאפל	**falafel**	falafel, fried chick pea balls in pitta bread with salad and hot pepper sauce
המבורגר	**hamburger**	hamburger
נקניקיה	**naknikiya**	hot dog, Frankfurter
חומוס	**KHumus**	humous (chick peas or ground chick pea paste) served with pitta bread and salad
פשטידה	**pashtida**	pie
כריך	**kariKH**	sandwich
סנדוויץ'	**sendvich**	sandwich
טחינה	**teKHina**	sesame seed paste
פיצה	**pitza**	pizza

CULINARY METHODS OF PREPARATION

אפוי	**afuy**	baked
מאפה	**ma'afeh**	baked
מבושל	**mevushal**	cooked, prepared
מטוגן	**metugan**	fried
בגריל	**be-gril**	grilled
בתנור	**ba-tanur**	oven-baked

70

מחית	**meKHit**	purée
נא	**na**	raw, rare
על האש	**al ha-'esh**	roasted, barbecued
מתובל	**metubal**	seasoned, spicy
צלוי	**tzalui**	stewed
ממולא	**memula**	stuffed, filled

MISCELLANEOUS

מנה	**mana**	dish, serving, course
חריף	**KHarif**	hot, spicy
מלוח	**maluaKH**	salty
תוספות	**tosafot**	side dishes
חמוץ	**KHamutz**	sour
מר	**mar**	sour
מתוק	**matok**	sweet
עלי גפן	**alay gefen**	vine leaves

SHOPPING

Israel has large, sophisticated, air-conditioned department stores and shopping malls. You'll also find exotic and colourful outdoor markets, called **shuk** (שוק), which offer anything from spices to antiques. They're also the best place to buy fruit and vegetables. Bargaining is customary in the **shuk**: if you begin by offering half the required price, you will probably get a fair deal. Do not, however, try to bargain in Tel Aviv's upmarket boutiques! In Jerusalem, it's advisable to seek advice about the current political situation before shopping in the eastern part of the city.

Some smaller shops and offices open at 8 or 9 a.m., close for a lunch break at around 1 p.m., and then re-open until 7 p.m.

USEFUL WORDS AND PHRASES

audio equipment	מערכות סטריאו	ma'araKHot sterio
baker	מאפיה	ma'afiya
bookshop	חנות ספרים	KHanut sfarim
boutique	בוטיק	butik
butcher	אטליז	itliz
to buy	לקנות	liknot
cake shop	קונדיטוריה	kondeturya
carrier bag (plastic)	שקית ניילון	sakit nailon
cheap	זול	zol
chemist	בית מרקחת	bayt mirkaKHat
department store	חנות כלבו	KHanut kolbo
diamond	יהלום	yahalom
fashion	אופנה	ofna
fishmonger	מוכר דגים	moKHer dagim
florist	מוכר פרחים	moKHer praKHim
goldsmith	צורף זהב	tzoref zahav
grocer	מכולת	makolet
hardware store	חנות כלי בית	KHanut klay bayit
ladies' wear	בגדי נשים	bigday nashim

72

menswear	בגדי גברים	bigday gvarim
newsagent	מוכר עתונים	moKHer itonim
receipt	קבלה	kabala
record and cassette shop	חנות תקליטים	KHanut taklitim
rug	שטיח	shatiaKH
sale	מכירה	meKHira
shoe shop	חנות נעליים	KHanut na'alayim
shop	חנות	KHanut
shop assistant	מוכר	moKHer (m)
	מוכרת	moKHeret (f)
to go shopping	לעשות קניות	la'asot kniyot
silversmith	צורף כסף	tzoref kesef
souvenir shop	חנות מזכרות	KHanut mazkarot
special offer	מבצע	mivtza
to spend	להוציא	lehotzi
stationer	חנות מכשירי כתיבה	KHanut maKHshiray ktiva
supermarket	שופרסל, סופרמרקט	supersal, supermarket
tailor	חייט	KHayat
till	קופה	kupa
toyshop	חנות צעצועים	KHanut tza'atzu'im
travel agent	סוכן נסיעות	soKHen nesi'ot
trolley	עגלה	agala

I'd like ...
אני מבקש/מבקשת ...
ani mevakesh *(m)*/mevakeshet *(f)* ...

Do you have ...?
יש לך ...?
yesh leKHa *(to a man)* ...?

יש לך ...?
yesh laKH *(to a woman)* ...?

73

How much is this?
כמה זה עולה?
<u>ka</u>ma zeh o<u>leh</u>?

That's too much
זה יותר מדי
zeh yo<u>ter</u> mi<u>dai</u>

I'll give you ...
אתן לך ...
<u>eten</u> le<u>KHa</u> *(to a man)* ...
אתן לך ...
<u>eten</u> laKH *(to a woman)* ...

That's my best offer
זה המקסימום
zeh ha-<u>maximum</u>

Two for ...
שניים ב...
<u>shnayim</u> be-...

OK, I'll take it
בסדר, אני לוקח/לוקחת
be<u>seder</u>, <u>ani</u> loke<u>aKH</u> *(m)*/lo<u>kaKHat</u> *(f)*

Can you gift-wrap it, please?
עטיפת מתנה, בבקשה
ati<u>fat</u> ma<u>tana</u>, beva<u>kasha</u>

Could you wrap it for me?
אפשר לעטוף את זה?
ef<u>shar</u> la'a<u>tof</u> et zeh?

Where is the ... department?
איפה מחלקת ה...?
<u>ay</u>fo maKH<u>le</u>ket ha-...?

Do you have any more of these?
יש עוד כאלה?
yesh od ka-<u>e</u>leh?

I'd like to change this please
אני מבקש/מבקשת להחליף את זה
<u>a</u>ni mevak<u>esh</u> *(m)*/mevak<u>eshet</u> *(f)* lehaKHl<u>if</u> et zeh

Have you anything larger/smaller/cheaper?
יש יותר גדול/קטן/זול?
yesh yo<u>ter</u> gad<u>ol</u>/ka<u>tan</u>/zol?

Does it come in other colours?
יש צבעים אחרים?
yesh tzva'<u>im</u> aKH<u>erim</u>?

Can I have a receipt?
אפשר לקבל קבלה?
ef<u>shar</u> leka<u>bel</u> kaba<u>la</u>?

Can I have a bag, please?
אפשר לקבל שקית, בבקשה?
ef<u>shar</u> leka<u>bel</u> sa<u>kit</u>, bevaka<u>sha</u>?

Can I try it/them on?
אפשר למדוד?
ef<u>shar</u> lim<u>dod</u>?

Where do I pay?
איפה אפשר לשלם?
<u>ay</u>fo ef<u>shar</u> lesha<u>lem</u>?

Can I have a refund?
אפשר לקבל החזר תשלום?
ef<u>shar</u> leka<u>bel</u> heKh<u>zer</u> tash<u>lum</u>?

75

I'm just looking
אני רק מסתכל/מסתכלת
<u>a</u>ni rak mista<u>kel</u> *(m)*/mista<u>kelet</u> *(f)*

I'll come back later
אני אחזור יותר מאוחר
<u>a</u>ni a<u>KHazor</u> yo<u>ter</u> me'u<u>KHar</u>

THINGS YOU'LL SEE

מאפיה	**ma'afiya**	bakery
מציאה	**metzi'a**	bargain
חנות ספרים	**KHanut sfarim**	bookshop
אטליז	**itliz**	butcher
קונדיטוריה	**kondeturya**	cake shop
מחלקה	**maKHlaka**	department
חנות כלבו	**KHanut kolbo**	department store
מכירת סוף העונה	**meKHirat sof ha-'ona**	end of season sale
אופנה	**ofna**	fashion
חומרי ניקוי לבית	**KHomray nikui la-bayit**	household cleaning materials
גלידריה	**glideriya**	ice cream shop
כשר	**kasher**	kosher
בגדי נשים	**bigday nashim**	ladies' clothing
מחלקת נשים	**maKHleket nashim**	ladies' department
קומת קרקע	**komat karka**	lower floor
שוק	**shuk**	market
בגדי גברים	**bigday gvarim**	menswear
לא מקבלים המחאות	**lo mekablim hamKHa'ot**	no cheques
נא לא לנעת	**na lo laga'at**	please do not touch

→

מחיר	**meкнir**	price
מוזל	**muzal**	reduced
השכרה	**haskara**	rental
מכירה	**meкhira**	sale
שירות עצמי	**sherut atzmi**	self-service
חנות נעליים	**кнanut na'alayim**	shoe shop
מבצע	**mivtza**	special offer
מוכר סיגריות	**moкнer sigariot**	tobacconist
צעצועים	**tza'atzu'im**	toys
סוכן נסיעות	**soкнen nesi'ot**	travel agent
קומה עליונה	**koma elyona**	upper floor
ירקות	**yerakot**	vegetables

THINGS YOU'LL HEAR

efshar la'azor leкнa *(to a man)*/**laкн?** *(to a woman)*
May I help you?

yesh leкнa *(to a man)*/**laкн** *(to a woman)* **kesef yoter katan?**
Have you anything smaller?

sliкнa, nigmar lanu
I'm sorry we're out of stock

zeh kol ma she-yesh
This is all we have

od mashehu?/zeh ha-kol?
Will there be anything else?

AT THE HAIRDRESSER

USEFUL WORDS AND PHRASES

appointment	תוֹר	tor
beard	זָקָן	za<u>kan</u>
blond	בְּלוֹנְד	blond
blow dry	פֶן	fen
brush *(noun)*	מִבְרֶשֶׁת	miv<u>re</u>shet
(verb)	לְהַבְרִישׁ	lehav<u>rish</u>
comb *(noun)*	מַסְרֵק	mas<u>rek</u>
(verb)	לְסָרֵק	lesa<u>rek</u>
conditioner	קוֹנְדִישׁוֹנֶר	kondishoner
curl	סִלְסוּל	sil<u>sul</u>
curlers	רוֹלִים	ro<u>lim</u>
curly	מְסוּלְסָל	mesul<u>sal</u>
dark	כֵּהֶה	<u>keheh</u>
dye *(noun)*	צֶבַע	<u>tzeva</u>
(verb)	לִצְבּוֹעַ	litz<u>bo</u>'a
fringe	פוֹנִי	<u>poni</u>
gel	גֵ'ל	jel
hair	שֵׂיעָר	say'<u>ar</u>
haircut	תִּסְפּוֹרֶת	tis<u>poret</u>
hairdresser	סַפָּר	sapar *(m)*
	סַפָּרִית	sapa<u>rit</u> *(f)*
hairdryer	מְיַבֵּשׁ שֵׂיעָר	maya<u>besh</u> say'<u>ar</u>
highlights	פַּסִים, גְּוונִים	pasim, gva<u>nim</u>
long	אָרוֹךְ	aro<u>KH</u>
moustache	שָׂפָם	sa<u>fam</u>
parting	שְׁבִיל	shvil
perm	פֶרְמָנֶנְט	<u>permanent</u>
shampoo	שַׁמְפּוּ	sham<u>po</u>
shave	גִּילוּחַ	giluа<u>KH</u>
shaving foam	קֶצֶף גִּילוּחַ	<u>ketzef</u> gilu<u>a</u>KH
short	קָצָר	ka<u>tzar</u>
styling mousse	מוּס	mus

78

I'd like to make an appointment
אפשר בבקשה להזמין תור?
efshar bevakasha lehazmin tor?

Just a trim please
רק ליישר, בבקשה
rak layasher, bevakasha

Not too much off
לא להוריד יותר מדי
lo lehorid yoter midai

A bit more off here please
אפשר להוריד עוד קצת פה, בבקשה?
efshar lehorid od ktzat po, bevakasha?

I'd like a cut and blow-dry
תספורת ופן, בבקשה
tisporet ve-fen, bevakasha

I'd like a perm
פרמננט, בבקשה
permanent, bevakasha

I'd like highlights
גוונים, בבקשה
gvanim, bevakasha

AT THE HAIRDRESSER

THINGS YOU'LL SEE

ספר	**sapar**	barber, men's hairdresser
מספרה	**maspera**	hairdresser
סלון	**salon**	hairdressing salon
עיצוב שיער	**itzuv say'ar**	hair styling, hairdresser
גברות	**gvarot**	(for) ladies
גברים	**gvarim**	(for) men

THINGS YOU'LL HEAR

ayKH tir<u>tzeh</u> et zeh?
How would you like it? *(to a man)*

ayKH tir<u>tzi</u> et zeh?
How would you like it? *(to a woman)*

zeh mas<u>pik</u> kat<u>zar</u>?
Is that short enough?

ata rot<u>zeh</u> kon<u>di</u>shoner?
Would you like any conditioner? *(to a man)*

at rot<u>za</u> kon<u>di</u>shoner?
Would you like any conditioner? *(to a woman)*

SPORT

Israel's most popular sports are football and basketball. In recent years tennis has been gaining ground, and so have water sports – diving, sailing, windsurfing and water skiing. Quality hotels and sports centres offer squash and weight-lifting facilities. There are many walking trails all over the country, rock climbing is offered in the Judean desert, and Mount Hermon has a small ski resort open in the mid-winter months. Cycling is possible, although there are very few designated routes, and drivers' courtesy leaves much to be desired. Israel has only one golf course, located near Caesaria.

There is, however, no shortage of swimming pools and developed bathing beaches. The swimming season in the Mediterranean is from spring to October, while Eilat caters for bathers all year round. Topless bathing is acceptable in Eilat and on some Mediterranean beaches, though not in urban locations; look around you to work out what the local norms are. It's advisable to swim only when a lifeguard is in attendance. A flag warning system operates on most beaches: black for absolutely no swimming, red for caution, and white (or blue and white) for all-clear.

Israel's climate is hot, and dehydration is an ever-imminent danger. During all sports activities, make sure you take plenty of drinks and wear a hat when in the sun.

USEFUL WORDS AND PHRASES

athletics	אתלטיקה	atletika
ball	כדור	kadur
beach	חוף	KHof
(for bathing)	חוף רחצה	KHof raKHatza
bicycle	אופניים	ofanayim
canoe	קנו	kanu
deckchair	כסא נוח	kiseh noaKH
diving *(underwater)*	צלילה	tzlila
diving board	קרש קפיצה	keresh kfitza

diving suit	חליפת צלילה	KHalifat tzlila
fishing	דיג	dayig
flippers	סנפירים	snapirim
football	כדורגל	kaduregel
football match	משחק כדורגל	misKHak kaduregel
goggles	משקפי שחיה	mishkafay sKHiya
golf	גולף	golf
golf course	אתר גולף	atar golf
gymnastics	התעמלות	hit'amlut
hockey	הוקי	hoki
jogging	ג'וגינג, ריצה	joging, ritza
lessons	שיעורים	shi'urim
mountaineering	טיפוס הרים	tipus harim
oxygen bottles	בקבוקי חמצן	bakbukay KHamtzan
pedal boat	סירת דוושות	sirat davshot
racket	רקטה, מחבט	maKHbet, raketa
riding	רכיבה	reKHiva
rowing boat	סירת משוטים	sirat mashotim
to run	לרוץ	larutz
sailboard	גלשן רוח	galshan ruaKH
sailing	שיט	shayit
sand	חול	KHol
sea	ים	yam
ski	סקי	ski
snorkel	שנורקל	shnorkel
stadium	אצטדיון	itztadyon
sunshade	שמשיה	shimshiya
surfboard	גלשן	galshan
to swim	לשחות	lisKHot
swimming pool	בריכת שחיה	brayKHat sKHiya
tennis	טניס	tenis
tennis court	מגרש טניס	migrash tenis
tennis racket	רקטה, מחבט טניס	maKHbet tenis, raketa
tent	אוהל	ohel
volleyball	כדור עף	kadur af
walking	הליכה	haliKHa
water-skiing	סקי מים	ski mayim

water skis	מגלשי סקי מים	miglashay ski mayim
wave	גל	gal
wind	רוח	ruaKH
windsurf	גלשן רוח	galshan ruaKH
yacht	יכטה	yaKHta

How do I get to the beach?
איך מגיעים לחוף?
ayKH magi'im la-KHof?

How deep is the water here?
מה עומק המים כאן?
ma omek ha-mayim kan?

Is there a swimming pool here?
יש כאן בריכת שחיה?
yesh kan brayKHat sKHiya?

Is the swimming pool heated?
הבריכה מחוממת?
ha-brayKHa meKHumemet?

Is it safe to swim here?
בטוח לשחות כאן?
batuaKH lisKHot kan?

Can I hire a deck chair/sunshade?
אפשר לשכור כסא נוח/שמשיה?
efshar liskor kiseh noaKH/shimshiya?

How much does it cost per hour/day?
כמה זה עולה לשעה/ליום?
kama zeh oleh le-sha'a/le-yom?

SPORT

Can I take water-skiing lessons?
אפשר לקבל שיעורים בסקי מים?
ef<u>shar</u> leka<u>bel</u> shi'u<u>rim</u> be-<u>ski</u> <u>ma</u>yim?

Where can I hire ...?
איפה אפשר לשכור ... ?
<u>ay</u>fo ef<u>shar</u> lis<u>kor</u> ... ?

THINGS YOU'LL SEE

חוף רחצה (מורשה)	<u>KH</u>of ra<u>KH</u>a<u>tza</u> (mur<u>sheh</u>)	(authorized) bathing beach
סירות	<u>si</u>rot	boats
חוף	<u>KH</u>of	beach, coast, shore
אופניים	ofa<u>na</u>yim	bicycles
מגרש	mig<u>rash</u>	court, sports field
ציוד	tzi<u>yud</u>	equipment
עזרה ראשונה	<u>ez</u>ra risho<u>na</u>	first aid
להשכרה	le-haska<u>ra</u>	for hire
אסור ל...	a<u>sur</u> le/li- ...	it is forbidden to ...
מרינה	ma<u>ri</u>na	marina
אסור לצלול	a<u>sur</u> litz<u>lol</u>	no diving
אסור לשחות	a<u>sur</u> lis<u>KH</u>ot	no swimming
מתקני ספורט	mitka<u>nay</u> sport	sporting facilities
מרכז ספורט	mer<u>kaz</u> sport	sports centre
אצטדיון	itztad<u>yon</u>	stadium
השחיה אסורה	ha-s<u>KH</u>i<u>ya</u> asu<u>ra</u>	swimming prohibited
מגרש טניס	mig<u>rash</u> <u>te</u>nis	tennis court
כרטיסים	karti<u>sim</u>	tickets
ספורט מים	sport <u>ma</u>yim	water sports

POST OFFICES AND BANKS

Post offices can be recognised by the word דואר (**doar**) meaning 'post' and by the symbol of a deer. Letter boxes are usually red and similar to those in Britain. In some large cities, you'll also see yellow letter boxes which are intended for local mail only. Post offices in Israel are open every morning between approximately 8.30 a.m. and 12 noon and most are open in the afternoons from 3.30 to 6 p.m. except on Fridays. Many post offices are closed for one additional afternoon a week. Israelis use the post office not only to buy stamps and send parcels, but to pay bills and purchase telephone tokens and phonecards (see TELEPHONES p 89). The main post offices in large cities have a poste restante and a telephone service for calling abroad since most payphones cannot be used for overseas calls.

Banks in Israel are open every morning and in the afternoon from 4 to 5.30 p.m. The Israeli unit of currency is the shekel (**shekel** שקל) which is divided into 100 agorot (singular **agora** אגורה). If you want to change shekels back into foreign currency, it is advisable to plan your purchase in advance.

USEFUL WORDS AND PHRASES

agora	אגורה	agora
agorot	אגורות	agorot
airmail	דואר אוויר	doar avir
bank	בנק	bank
banknote	שטר כסף	shtar kesef
to change	להחליף, להמיר	lehaKHlif, lehamir
cheque	שק, צ׳ק	shek, chek
collection	איסוף דואר	isuf doar
counter	דלפק, אשנב	dalpak, eshnav
customs form	טופס מכס	tofes meKHes
delivery	חלוקה	KHaluka
deposit	הפקדה	hafkada

English	Hebrew	Transliteration
exchange rate	שער חליפין	sha'ar KHalifin
form	טופס	tofes
international money order	המחאת כסף בינלאומית	hamKHa'at kesef baynle'umit
letter	מכתב	miKHtav
letter box	תיבת מכתבים	tayvat miKHtavim
mail	דואר	doar
money	כסף	kesef
money order	המחאת כסף	hamKHa'at kesef
overseas	חו"ל, לחו"ל	KHul, le-KHul
package, parcel	חבילה	KHavila
P.O. box	תיבת דואר	tayvat doar
post	דואר	doar
postage rates	דמי דואר, מחיר משלוח	dmay doar, meKHir mishloaKH
postal order	המחאת דואר	hamKHa'at doar
postcard	גלויה	gluya
postcode	מיקוד	mikud
poste restante	דואר שמור	doar shamur
postman	דוור	davar
post office	סניף דואר	snif doar
pound sterling	לירה שטרלינג	lira sterling
registered letter	מכתב רשום	miKHtav rashum
shekel	שקל	shekel
stamp	בול	bul
surface mail	דואר ים	doar yam
telegram	מברק	mivrak
traveller's cheque	המחאת נוסעים	hamKHa'at nos'im

How much is a letter/postcard to …?
כמה עולה לשלוח מכתב/גלויה ל...?
kama oleh lishloaKH miKHtav/gluya le-...?

I would like a stamp for a postcard to England
אפשר לקבל בול לגלויה לאנגליה?
efshar lekabel bul le-gluya le-angliya?

I want to register this letter
אבקש לשלוח מכתב זה בדואר רשום
avakesh lishloaKH miKHtav zeh be-doar rashum

I want to send this parcel to ...
אבקש לשלוח חבילה זאת ל-...
avakesh lishloaKH KHavila zot le-...

Where can I post this?
איפה אפשר לשלוח את זה?
ayfo efshar lishloaKH et zeh?

Is there any mail for me?
יש דואר בשבילי?
yesh doar bishvili?

I'd like to send a telegram
אבקש לשלוח מברק
avakesh lishloaKH mivrak

This is to go airmail
דואר אוויר בבקשה
doar avir bevakasha

I'd like to change this into ...
אבקש להחליף את זה ל-...
avakesh lehaKHlif et zeh le-...

Can I cash these traveller's cheques?
אפשר להמיר את המחאות הנוסעים האלה?
efshar lehamir et hamKHa'ot ha-nos'im ha-eleh?

What is the exchange rate for the pound?
מה שער החליפין ללירה שטרלינג?
ma sha'ar ha-KHalifin la-lira sterling?

POST OFFICES AND BANKS

THINGS YOU'LL SEE

Hebrew	Transliteration	English
מען, כתובת	ma'an, ketovet	address
נמען	nim'an	addressee
דואר אוויר	doar avir	airmail
בנק	bank	bank
החלפת מטבע זר	hakHlafat matbe'a zar	bureau de change
איסוף דואר	isuf doar	collection times
דואר אקספרס, דואר מהיר	doar ekspres, doar mahir	express
בול בתוך הארץ	bul betoKH ha-aretz	inland postage
הרקה אחרונה	haraka aKHrona	last collection
מכתב	miKHtav	letter
תיבת דואר, תיבת מכתבים	tayvat doar, tayvat miKHtavim	letter box
המחאות כסף	hamKHa'ot kesef	money orders
שעות פתיחה	sha'ot petiKHa	opening hours
דלפק חבילות	dalpak KHavilot	parcels counter
מחיר משלוח, דמי דואר	meKHir mishloaKH, dmay doar	postage
בול לחו"ל, מחיר משלוח לחו"ל	bul le-KHul, meKHir mishloaKH le-KHul	postage abroad
מיקוד	mikud	postcode
דואר שמור	doar shamur	poste restante
דואר	doar	post office
דואר רשום	doar rashum	registered mail
שולח	sholeaKH	sender
בולים	bulim	stamps
מברקים	mivrakim	telegrams

88

TELEPHONES

Israel's telephone network is run by a government-controlled company, **bezek** (בזק), which is gradually improving a dated and over-congested system. Pay-phones are operated with special tokens, **asimonim** (singular: **asimon** אסימון), which can be bought singly or in packs of ten from vending machines, post offices, and many kiosks and shops. Have at least five to hand for a local call. Card-operated phones are currently being introduced. Direct dialling is available to most countries. Many pay-phones are still not equipped for dialling abroad, unless you ask the operator for a reverse charge call. International calls can be made from some pay-phones, and from private telephones or central post offices.

USEFUL WORDS AND PHRASES

call	שיחת טלפון	siKHat telefon
to call	לטלפן	letalpen
code	קידומת	kidomet
crossed line	תקלה בקוים	takala ba-kavim
to dial	לחייג	leKHayeg
dialling tone	צליל חיוג	tzlil KHiyug
emergency	מקרי חירום	mikray KHerum
enquiries	מודיעין	modi'in
extension	שלוחה	shluKHa
international call	שיחה בינלאומית	siKHa baynle'umit
local call	שיחה מקומית	siKHa mekomit
long-distance call	שיחה בין עירונית	siKHa bayn ironit
number	מספר	mispar
operator	מרכזיה	merkaziya
pay-phone	טלפון ציבורי	telefon tziburi
phonecard	טלקרד	telecard
receiver	שפופרת	shfoferet

reverse charge call	גוביינא, קולקט	govaina, kolekt
telephone	טלפון	telefon
telephone box	תא טלפון	ta telefon
telephone directory	מדריך טלפון	madriKH telefon
telephone token	אסימון	asimon
wrong number	טעות במספר	ta'ut ba-mispar

Where is the nearest phone box?
איפה תא הטלפון הקרוב?
ayfo ta ha-telefon ha-karov?

Can I have a token for the phone?
אפשר לקבל אסימון?
efshar lekabel asimon?

Is there a telephone directory?
יש מדריך טלפון?
yesh madriKH telefon?

I would like the directory for ...
אפשר לקבל את המדריך לאיזור ... ?
efshar lekabel et ha-madriKH le-ayzor ... ?

Can I call abroad from here?
אפשר לטלפן מכאן לחו״ל?
efshar letalpen mikan le-KHul?

How much is a call to ...?
כמה עולה שיחה ל...?
kama ola siKHa le-... ?

I would like to reverse the charges
אבקש לטלפן קולקט
avakesh letalpen kolekt

I would like a number in ...
אבקש למצוא מספר ב...
avakesh limtzo mispar be-...

Hello, this is ... speaking
שלום, מדבר/מדברת ...
shalom, medaber *(m)*/medaberet *(f)* ...

Is that ...?
זה/זו ...?
zeh *(to a man)*/zo *(to a woman)* ...?

Speaking
מדבר/מדברת
medaber *(m)*/medaberet *(f)*

May I speak to ... ?
אפשר לדבר עם ...?
efshar ledaber im ... ?

Extension ... please
שלוחה ..., בבקשה
shluKHa ..., bevakasha

Please tell him/her ... called
בבקשה למסור ל/חלה ש... טלפן
bevakasha limsor lo/la she-... tilpen *(if a man called)*

בבקשה למסור ל/חלה ש... טלפנה
bevakasha limsor lo/la she-... tilpena *(if a woman called)*

Ask him to call me back please
אפשר לבקש שיחזור צלצול, בבקשה?
efshar levakesh she-yaKHzir tziltzul, bevakasha?

My number is ...
המספר שלי הוא ...
hamispar sheli hu ...

TELEPHONES

Do you know where he is?
אתה יודע איפה הוא?
<u>a</u>ta yo<u>de</u>'a <u>ay</u>fo hu? *(to a man)*

את יודעת איפה הוא?
at yo<u>da</u>'at <u>ay</u>fo hu? *(to a woman)*

When will he be back?
מתי הוא יחזור?
ma<u>tai</u> hu ya<u>KHzor</u>?

Could you leave a message?
אפשר להשאיר הודעה?
ef<u>shar</u> lehash'<u>ir</u> hoda'<u>a</u>?

I'll ring back later
אתקשר שוב אחר כך
etka<u>sher</u> shuv a<u>KHar</u> ka<u>KH</u>

Sorry, wrong number
סליחה, טעות במספר
sli<u>KH</u>a, ta'<u>ut</u> bamis<u>par</u>

THINGS YOU'LL SEE

בזק	**bezek**	Bezek
חיוג ישיר	**KHiyug yashir**	direct dialling
חירום	**KHerum**	emergency
מודיעין	**modi'in**	enquiries
שירות תיקונים	**shayrut tikunim**	faults service
מרכזיה	**merkaziya**	operator
מקולקל	**mekulkal**	out of order
בינלאומי	**baynle'umi**	international
טלפון	**telefon**	telephone

REPLIES YOU MAY BE GIVEN

et mi ata rotzeh? *(to a man)*
et mi at rotza? *(to a woman)*
Who would you like to speak to?

ta'ut ba-mispar
You've got the wrong number

mi medaber *(to a man)*/**medaberet** *(to a woman)*?
Who's speaking?

ma ha-mispar shelKHa *(to a man)*/**shelaKH** *(to a woman)*?
What is your number?

hu lo nimtza/hi lo nimtzet
He's not in/she's not in

hu yaKHzor be-...
He'll be back at ... o'clock

hi taKHzor be-...
She'll be back at ... o'clock

titkasher *(to a man)*/**titkashri** *(to a woman)* **shuv maKHar**
Please call again tomorrow

ani agid lo/la she-tilpanta *(to a man)*
I'll tell him/her you called

ani agid lo/la she-tilpant *(to a woman)*
I'll tell him/her you called

HEALTH

Israel has a very high standard of health care; while the doctor's bedside manner may at times seem less than courteous, you can count on first-rate care in hospitals and clinics. All travellers must be insured to cover illness, accidents and any subsequent hospitalization. Most doctors practice in clinics called **kupat KHolim** (קופת חולים) where there are general practitioners as well as specialists. The public first-aid and ambulance service, **magen david adom** (מגן דוד אדום), should be contacted for emergencies.

All fruit and vegetables should be washed thoroughly to avoid any stomach problems. If travelling in summer, the sun can be extremely dangerous, particularly for fair-skinned Europeans and North Americans. It is advisable to wear a hat when in the sun and drink plenty of fluids to avoid sunstroke and dehydration.

USEFUL WORDS AND PHRASES

accident	תאונה	te'una
ambulance	אמבולנס	ambulans
anaemic	אנמי	anemi
appendicitis	דלקת תוספתן, אפנדיציט	daleket toseftan, apenditzit
asthma	אסתמה	astma
backache	כאב גב	ke'ev gav
bandage	תחבושת	taKHboshet
bite (by dog)	נשיכה	neshiKHa
(by insect)	עקיצה	akitza
bladder	שלפוחית	shalpuKHit
blood	דם	dam
blood donor	תורם דם	torem dam
burn	כוויה	keviya
cancer	סרטן	sartan
chemist	בית מרקחת	bayt mirkaKHat
chest	חזה	KHazeh

94

chickenpox	אבעבועות רוח	aba'abu'ot ruaKH
cholera	חולירע	KHolira
clinic	מרפאה	mirpa'ah
cold	הצטננות	hitztanenut
concussion	זעזוע מוח	za'azu'a moaKH
constipation	עצירות	atzirut
corn	יבלת	yabelet
cough	שיעול	shi'ul
cut	חתך	KHataKH
dentist	רופא שניים	rofeh shinayim (m)
	רופאת שניים	rof'at shinayim (f)
diabetes	סכרת	sakeret
diarrhoea	קלקול קיבה	kilkul kayva
dizziness	סחרחורת	sKHarKHoret
doctor	רופא	rofeh (m)
	רופאה	rof'ah (f)
(form of address)	דוקטור	doktor
earache	כאב אוזניים	ke'ev oznayim
fever	חום	KHom
filling	סתימה	stima
first aid	עזרה ראשונה	ezra rishona
flu	שפעת	shapa'at
fracture	שבר	shever
gastroenteritis	דלקת קיבה	daleket kayva
German measles	אדמת	ademet
haemorrhage	דימום	dimum
hayfever	קדחת השחת,	kadaKHat ha-shaKHat,
	אלרגיה	elergia
headache	כאב ראש	ke'ev rosh
heart	לב	lev
heart attack	התקף לב	hetkef lev
hospital	בית חולים	bayt KHolim
ill	חולה	KHoleh (m), KHolah (f)
indigestion	קלקול קיבה	kilkul kayva
kidney	כליה	klaya
lump	גוש	gush
malaria	קדחת	kadaKHat

measles	חצבת	KHatzevet
migraine	מיגרנה, כאב ראש	migrena, ke'ev rosh
mumps	חזרת	KHazeret
nausea	בחילה	beKHila
nurse	אח	aKH *(m)*
	אחות	aKHot *(f)*
operation	ניתוח	nituaKH
pain	כאב	ke'ev
penicillin	פניצילין	penitzilin
plaster *(sticky)*	פלסטר, אגד מדבק	plaster, eged medabek
plaster of Paris	גבס	geves
pneumonia	דלקת ריאות	daleket rayot
pregnant	בהריון	be-herayon
prescription	מרשם	mirsham
rheumatism	שיגרון	shigaron
scald	כוויה	keviya
scratch	סריטה	srita
sore throat	כאב גרון	ke'ev garon
splinter	קוץ	kotz
sting	עקיצה	akitza
stomach	בטן	beten
temperature	חום	KHom
tonsils	שקדים	shkedim
toothache	כאב שיניים	ke'ev shinayim
travel sickness	מחלת ים	maKHalat yam
ulcer	אולקוס	ulkus
vaccination	חיסון	KHisun
to vomit	להקיא	lehaki
whooping cough	שעלת	sha'elet
yellow fever	קדחת צהובה	kadaKHat tzehuba

I have a pain in ...
... יש לי כאבים ב
yesh li ke'evim ba-...

I don't feel well
אני מרגיש/מרגישה לא טוב
a̱ni margish *(m)*/margi̱sha *(f)* lo tov

I feel faint
אני מרגיש חלש
a̱ni margish KHalash *(m)*

אני מרגישה חלשה
a̱ni margi̱sha KHala̱sha *(f)*

I feel sick
יש לי בחילות
yesh li beKHilot

I feel dizzy
יש לי סחרחורת
yesh li sKHarKHoret

I need to go to the clinic
אני רוצה למרפאה
a̱ni rotzeh le-mirpa'a *(m)*

אני רוצה למרפאה
a̱ni rotza le-mirpa'a *(f)*

It hurts here
כואב לי פה
ko'ev li po

It's a sharp/dull pain
זה כאב חד/עמום
zeh ke'ev KHad/amum

It hurts all the time
כואב כל הזמן
ko'ev kol ha-zman

It only hurts now and then
כואב לפעמים
ko'ev lif'am<u>im</u>

It hurts when you touch it
כואב כשנוגעים
ko'ev ke-she-nog'<u>im</u>

It hurts more at night
כואב יותר בלילה
ko'ev yo<u>ter</u> ba-<u>lai</u>la

It stings
זה צורב
zeh tzo<u>rev</u>

It aches
כואב לי
ko'<u>ev</u> li

I have a temperature
יש לי חום
yesh li KHom

I need a prescription for ...
אני צריך/צריכה מרשם ל...
<u>a</u>ni tza<u>riKH</u> *(m)*/tzri<u>KHa</u> *(f)* mir<u>sham</u> le-...

I normally take ...
אני בדרך כלל לוקח ...
<u>a</u>ni be-<u>de</u>reKH klal lo<u>kea</u>KH ... *(m)*

אני בדרך כלל לוקחת ...
<u>a</u>ni be-<u>de</u>reKH klal lo<u>ka</u>KHat ... *(f)*

I'm allergic to ...
יש לי אלרגיה ל...
yesh li a<u>ler</u>gia le-...

Have you got anything for ...?
?...יש משהו ל
yesh <u>ma</u>-she-hu le-...?

Do I need a prescription for ...?
?...צריך מרשם ל
tzari<u>KH</u> mir<u>sham</u> le-...?

I have lost a filling
אבדה לי סתימה
av<u>da</u> li sti<u>ma</u>

THINGS YOU'LL SEE

אמבולנס	**ambulans**	ambulance
מרפאה	**mirpa'ah**	clinic
רופא שניים	**rofeh shinayim**	dentist *(m)*
רופאת שניים	**rof'at shinayim**	dentist *(f)*
רופא	**rofeh**	doctor *(m)*
רופאה	**rof'ah**	doctor *(f)*
דוקטור (ד"ר)	**doktor**	doctor (Dr) *(title)*
רוקח	**rokeaKH**	duty chemist
תחנת עזרה ראשונה	**taKHanat ezra rishona**	first-aid post
קופת חולים	**kupat KHolim**	general health-care clinic
בית חולים	**bayt KHolim**	hospital
תרופה	**trufa**	medicine
בקיבה ריקה	**be-kayva rayka**	on an empty stomach
אופטיקאי	**optikai**	optician
מגן דוד אדום	**magen david adom**	public first-aid and ambulance service
מרפאה	**mirpa'ah**	surgery

99

THINGS YOU'LL HEAR

kakн *(to a man)*/**keкнi** *(to a woman)* ... **kadurim kol pa'am**
Take ... tablets at a time

im mayim
With water

pa'am aкнat be-yom
Once a day

pa'amayim be-yom
Twice a day

shalosh pe'amim be-yom
Three times a day

ma ata lokeaкн be-dereкн klal? *(to a man)*
ma at lokaкнat be-dereкн klal? *(to a woman)*
What do you normally take?

le-zeh tzariкн mirsham
For that you need a prescription

CONVERSION TABLES

DISTANCES

Distances are marked in kilometres. To convert kilometres to miles, divide the km. by 8 and multiply by 5 (one km. being five-eighths of a mile). Convert miles to km. by dividing the miles by 5 and multiplying by 8. A mile is 1609m. (1.609km.).

km.	miles *or* km.	miles
1.61	**1**	0.62
3.22	**2**	1.24
4.83	**3**	1.86
6.44	**4**	2.48
8.05	**5**	3.11
9.66	**6**	3.73
11.27	**7**	4.35
12.88	**8**	4.97
14.49	**9**	5.59
16.10	**10**	6.21

Other units of length:

1 centimetre = 0.39 in.	1 inch = 25.4 millimetres
1 metre = 39.37 in.	1 foot = 0.30 metre (30 cm.)
10 metres = 32.81 ft.	1 yard = 0.91 metre

WEIGHTS

The unit you will come into most contact with is the kilogram (kilo), equivalent to 2 lb 3 oz. To convert kg. to lbs., multiply by 2 and add one-tenth of the result (thus, 6 kg x 2 = 12 + 1.2, or 13.2 lbs). One ounce is about 28 grams, and 1 lb is 454 g.

CONVERSION TABLES

grams	ounces		ounces	grams
50	1.76		1	28.3
100	3.53		2	56.7
250	8.81		4	113.4
500	17.63		8	226.8

kg.	lbs. or kg.	lbs.
0.45	1	2.20
0.91	2	4.41
1.36	3	6.61
1.81	4	8.82
2.27	5	11.02
2.72	6	13.23
3.17	7	15.43
3.63	8	17.64
4.08	9	19.84
4.53	10	22.04

TEMPERATURE

To convert centigrade or Celsius degrees into Fahrenheit, the accurate method is to multiply the °C figure by 1.8 and add 32. Similarly, to convert °F to °C, subtract 32 from the °F figure and divide by 1.8. This will give you a truly accurate conversion, but takes a little time in mental arithmetic! See the table below.

°C	°F		°C	°F	
-10	14		25	77	
0	32		30	86	
5	41		36.9	98.4	body temperature
10	50		40	104	
20	68		100	212	boiling point

LIQUIDS

Motorists from the UK will be used to seeing petrol priced per litre (and may even know that one litre is about $1\frac{3}{4}$ pints). One 'imperial' gallon is roughly $4\frac{1}{2}$ litres, but USA drivers must remember that the American gallon is only 3.8 litres (1 litre = 1.06 US quart). In the following table, imperial gallons are used:

litres	gals. or l.	gals.
4.54	1	0.22
9.10	2	0.44
13.64	3	0.66
18.18	4	0.88
22.73	5	1.10
27.27	6	1.32
31.82	7	1.54
36.37	8	1.76
40.91	9	1.98
45.46	10	2.20
90.92	20	4.40
136.38	30	6.60
181.84	40	8.80
227.30	50	11.00

TYRE PRESSURES

lb/sq.in.	15	18	20	22	24
kg/sq.cm.	1.1	1.3	1.4	1.5	1.7

lb/sq.in.	26	28	30	33	35
kg/sq.cm.	1.8	2.0	2.1	2.3	2.5

MINI-DICTIONARY

about: about 16 be-ereKH shesh esreh
accelerator davshat ha-delek
accident te'una
accommodation megurim
ache ke'ev
adaptor *(electrical)* ma'avir KHashmali
address ktovet
adhesive niyar devek
after aKHaray
aftershave after shayv
again od pa'am
against *(opposing)* neged
air-conditioning mizug avir
aircraft matos
air freshener metaher avir
air hostess dayelet
airline KHevrat te'ufa
airport sdeh te'ufa
alcohol mashkeh KHarif
all kol
  all the streets kol ha-reKHovot
  that's all, thanks zeh ha-kol, toda
almost kim'at
alone levad
already kvar
always tamid
am: I am ani
ambulance ambulans
America amerika
American *(man, adj)* amerika'i *(woman)* amerika'it
Amman rabat amon
ancient atik
and veh-...
ankle karsol
anorak me'il geshem kal

another *(different)* aKHer *(additional)* od
antique shop KHanut atikot
antiquities atikot
antiseptic (solution) KHomer KHitui
apartment dira
aperitif aperitif
appetite te'avon
apple tapuaKH etz
application form tofes bakasha
appointment pgisha *(medical)* tor
apricot mishmesh
Arab *(man, adj)* aravi *(woman)* araviya
Arabic aravit
archeological excavation KHafira arKHe'ologit
archeological site atar arKHe'ologi
are: you are ata *(to a man)/*at *(to a woman)*
  we are anaKHnu
  they are hem *(m)/*hen *(f)*
arm yad, zro'a
army tzava
art omanut
art gallery galeria le-omanut
artist oman
as: as soon as possible ba-mehirut ha-efsharit
ashtray ma'afera
asleep yashen
aspirin aspirin
at: at the post office ba-do'ar
  at night ba-laila
attractive yafeh
aubergine KHatzil
aunt doda

Australia ostralia
Australian *(man, adj)* ostrali
  (woman) ostralit
Austria ostria
away: is it far away? zeh
  raKHok?
  go away! leKH *(to a man)/*
  leKHi *(to a woman)* mipo!
awful nora
axe garzen
axle tzir

baby tinok *(m)*, tinoket *(f)*
back *(not front)* aKHor
  (body) gav
  (adj) aKHori
backgammon shesh besh
bad ra
bake le'efot
baker ofeh
balcony mirpeset
ball *(football etc)* kadur
ballpoint pen et kaduri
banana banana
band *(pop, rock)* lahaka
  (brass) tizmoret
bandage taKHboshet
bank bank
banknote shtar
bar bar
  bar of chocolate tavlat
  shokolad
barbecue barbekiu
bargain *(noun)* metzi'a
  (verb) la'amod al ha-mekaKH
basement martef
basin *(sink)* kior
basket sal
bath ambatia
  to have a bath la'asot ambatia
bathing beach KHof raKHatza
bathing hat kova raKHatza

bathroom KHadar ambatia
battery solela, bateria
bazaar bazar, shuk
beach KHof
beans sheu'it
beard zakan
because ki, biglal
bed mita
bed linen klay mita
bedroom KHadar shayna
beef basar bakar
beer bira
before lifnay, kodem
  before the summer lifnay
  ha-kayitz
  I was here before hayiti kan
  kodem
beginner matKHil *(m)*, matKHila *(f)*
behind ... me'aKHaray ...
  she was left behind hi nish'ara
  me'aKHor
beige bezH
Beirut bayrut
bell pa'amon
below lemata, mitaKHat
  he is waiting below hu meKHake
  lemata
  (it is) below zero mitaKHat la-efes
belt KHagora
beside al yad, leyad
best ha-tov bayoter
Bethlehem bayt leKHem
better tov yoter
between bayn
bicycle ofanayim
big gadol
bikini bikini
bill KHeshbon
bird tzipor
birthday yom huledet
  happy birthday! yom huledet
  samehaKH!

birthday present matnat yom huledet
biscuit *(sweet)* ugiya
 (savoury) kreker
bite *(noun: by dog)* neshiKHa
 (by insect) akitza
 (verb) linshoKH
bitter mar
black shaKHor
blackberry uKHmania
blanket smiKHa
bleach *(noun: for cleaning)* KHlor, malbin
 (verb: hair) lehavhir
blind *(cannot see)* iver
blister yabelet
blood dam
blouse KHultza
blue kaKHol
boat *(large)* sfina
 (small) sira
body guf
boil *(verb)* lehartiaKH
bolt *(noun: on door)* man'ul
 (verb) lin'ol
bone etzem
bonnet *(car)* miKHseh mano'a
book *(noun)* sefer
 (verb) lehazmin
booking office misrad kartisim
bookshop KHanut sfarim
boot *(car)* bagaZH
 (footwear) magaf
border gvul
boring mesha'amem
born: I was born in ... noladeti be-...
both: both of them shnayhem
 both of us shnaynu
 both ... and ... gam ... ve-gam ...
bottle bakbuk

bottle-opener potKHan bakbukim
bottom taKHtit
 (sea) karka'it
bowl ke'ara
box kufsa
boy *(young)* yeled
 (older) na'ar
boyfriend KHaver
bra KHaziya
bracelet tzamid
brake *(noun)* breks
 (verb) livlom
brandy brendi, koniak
bread leKHem
breakdown *(car)* pancher
 (nervous) hitmotetut atzabim
breakfast aruKHat boker
breathe linshom
 I can't breathe kasheh li linshom
bridge gesher
briefcase mizvada
British briti *(m)*, britit *(f)*
brochure *(tourist)* KHoveret mayda
broken shavur
 broken leg regel shvura
brooch sikat noy
brother aKH
brown KHum
bruise petza
brush *(noun)* mivreshet
 (verb) lehavrish
bucket dli
building binyan
bumper pagosh
burglar poretz
burn *(noun)* keviya
 (verb) lisrof
bus otobus
business esek
 it's none of your business zeh lo iskeKHa

bus station taKHanat otobus
busy *(person)* asuk (m), asuka (f)
  (crowded) so'en
but aval
butcher katzav
butter KHem'a
button kaftor
buy liknot
by: by the window leyad
  ha-KHalon
  by Friday ad yom shishi
  by myself levadi

cabbage kruv
café bayt kafeh
cagoule me'il geshem kal
Cairo kahir
cake uga
calculator maKHshev kis
call: what's it called? ayKH
  kor'im la-zeh?
camel gamal
camera matzlema
campsite kemping
camshaft mimseret
can *(tin)* paKHit
  can I have ...? efshar
  lekabel ...?
Canada kanada
Canadian *(man, adj)* kanadi
  (woman) kanadit
cancer sartan
candle ner
canoe kanu, kayak
cap *(bottle)* miKHseh
  (hat) kova
car meKHonit
caravan karavan
carburettor karburator
card kartis
cardigan sveder im kaftorim
careful zahir

be careful! zehirut!
carpet shatiaKH
carriage *(train)* karon
carrot gezer
carry-cot minsa le-tinok
case *(suitcase)* mizvada
cash mezumanim
  (coins) matbe'ot
  to pay cash leshalem bimzuman
cassette kaseta
cassette player tayp kasetot
castle tira
cat KHatul
cathedral katedrala
Catholic katoli (m), katolit (f)
cauliflower kruvit
cave me'ara
cemetery bayt kvarot
centre merkaz
certificate te'uda
chair kiseh
chambermaid KHadranit
chamber music musika kamerit
change *(noun: money returned)* odef
  (small) kesef katan
  (verb: clothes) le-haKHlif begadim
cheap zol
cheers! leKHayim!
cheese gvina
chemist *(shop)* bayt mirkaKHat
cheque chek
cheque book pinkas chekim
cherry duvdevan
chess shaKHmat
chest KHazeh
chewing gum mastik
chicken tarnegolet
  (meat) off
child yeled (m), yalda (f)
children yeladim (m), yeladot (f)
china KHarsina
China sin

Chinese *(man, adj)* sini
  (woman) sinit
chips chips
chocolate shokolad
  box of chocolates bonbonyera
chop *(food)* tzela
  (to cut) laKHtoKH
Christ yeshu
Christian notzri *(m)*, notzriya *(f)*
Christianity natzrut
Christian name shem prati
Christmas KHag ha-molad
church knesiya
cigar sigar
cigarette sigaria
cinema kolno'a
city ir
city centre merkaz ha-ir
classical music musika klasit
clean naki
clear *(obvious)* barur
  (water) tzalul
  is that clear? zeh barur?
clever KHaKHam
clock sha'on
  (alarm) sha'on me'orer
close *(near)* karov
  (stuffy) maKHnik
  (verb) lisgor
  the shop is closed ha-KHanut
  sgura
clothes bgadim
club mo'adon
  (cards) tiltan
clutch klach
coach *(bus)* otobus
  (of train) karon
coach station taKHana merkazit
coast KHof
coastal: the coastal plateau
  mishor ha-KHof
coat me'il

coathanger mitleh
cockroach juk
coffee kafeh
coin matbe'a
cold *(illness)* hitztanenut
  (adj) metzunan
collar tzavaron
collection *(stamps etc)* osef
colour tzeva
colour film seret tziv'oni
comb *(noun)* masrek
  (verb) lesarek
come lavo
  I come from … ani ba me-…
  (m)/ani ba'a me-… *(f)*
  we came last week banu ba-
  shavu'a she'avar
  come here! bo hena! *(to a
  man)*/bo'i hena! *(to a woman)*
compact disc compakt disk
compartment ta
complicated mesubaKH
computer maKHshev
computer disk disk maKHshev
concert kontzert
conditioner *(hair)* kondishoner
condom kondom
conductor *(bus)* mevaker kartisim
  (orchestra) menatze'aKH
congratulations! mazal tov!
constipation atzirut
consulate konsulia
contact lenses adashot maga
contraceptive emtza'i meni'a
cook *(noun)* tabaKH *(m)*, tabaKHit *(f)*
  (verb) levashel
cooking utensils klay bishul
cool karir
cork pkak
corkscrew KHoletz pkakim
corner pina
corridor misderon

cosmetics kosmetika
cost *(verb)* la'alot
　what does it cost? kama zeh oleh?
cotton kutna
cotton wool tzemer gefen
cough *(noun)* shi'ul
　(verb) lehishta'el
country *(state)* medina
　(not town) ezor kafri
cousin ben dod *(m)*, bat doda *(f)*
crab sartan
cramp hitkavtzut shririm
crayfish lobster
cream shamenet
　whipped cream katzefet
credit card kartis ashrai
crew tzevet
crisps chips
crowded tzafuf
cruise shayit
crutches kabayim
cry *(weep)* livkot
　(shout) litz'ok
cucumber melafefon
cufflinks KHafatim
cup sefel
cupboard aron
curlers rolim
curls taltalim
curry kari
curtain vilon
Customs meKHes
cut *(noun: injury)* srita
　(verb) laKHtoKH

dad aba
dairy *(adj)* KHalavi
　dairy products mutzray KHalav
damp laKH
dance *(noun)* rikud

dangerous mesukan
dark *(colour)* keheh
　(night) KHashuKH
date *(meeting)* pgisha
　(fruit) tamar
daughter bat
day yom
dead met
Dead Sea yam ha-melaKH
deaf KHeresh
dear yakar
deckchair kiseh noaKH
deep amok
deliberately be-KHavana
dentist rofeh shinayim
dentures shinayim totavot
deny lehakKHish
　I deny it ani makKHish *(m)/*
　makKHisha *(f)* et zeh
deodorant de'odorant
department store KHanut kolbo
departure yetzi'a, aziva
desert midbar
develop *(a film)* lefateaKH
diamond yahalom
diarrhoea kilkul kayva
diary yoman
dictionary milon
die lamut
diesel dizel
different: that's different zeh shoneh
　I'd like a different one ani rotzeh *(m)/*rotza *(f)* mashehu shoneh
difficult kasheh
dining car kron mis'ada
dining room KHadar oKHel
directory *(telephone)* madriKH telefon
dirty meluKHlaKH
disabled neKHeh
distributor *(car)* mafleg

109

dive *(verb)* litzlol
diving board keresh tzlila
divorced garush *(m)*, grusha *(f)*
do la'asot
doctor rofeh
document mismaKH
dog kelev
doll buba
dollar dolar
donkey KHamor
door delet
double room KHeder zugi
doughnut sufganya
down lemata
drawing pin na'atz
dress simla
drink *(noun)* mashkeh
 (verb) lishtot
 would you like a drink? ma
 tishteh *(to a man)*/tishti? *(to a
 woman)*
drinking water may shtiya
drive *(verb)* linhog
driver nehag *(m)*, naheget *(f)*
driving licence rishayon nehiga
drunk shikor
dry yavesh
dry cleaner nikui yavesh
dummy *(for baby)* motzetz
during bemesheKH
dustbin paKH ashpa
duster matlit avak
duty-free duty free

each *(every)* kol eKHad
 twenty shekels each esrim
 shekel le'eKHad
ear ozen
 ears oznayim
early mukdam
earrings agilim
east mizraKH

easy kal
eat le'eKHol
egg baytza
Egypt mitzrayim
Egyptian *(man, adj)* mitzri
 (woman) mitzrit
either: either of them zeh o zeh
 either ... or ... o ... o ...
elastic gamish
elastic band gumiya
elbow marpek
electric KHashmali
electricity KHashmal
else: something else mashehu
 aKHer
 someone else mishehu aKHer
 somewhere else makom aKHer
embarrassing meviKH
embassy shagrirut
embroidery rikma
emerald izmargad
emergency KHerum
empty rayk
end sof
engaged *(couple)* me'oras
 (occupied) tafus
engine *(motor)* mano'a
England anglia
English angli
 (language) anglit
Englishman angli
Englishwoman angliya
enlargement hagdala
enough maspik, dai
entertainment bidur
entrance knisa
envelope ma'atafa
escalator madregot na'ot
especially bimyukHad
evening erev
every kol
everyone kulam

everything ha-kol
everywhere be-KHol makom
example dugma
  for example le-dugma
excellent metzuyan
excess baggage mit'an odef
exchange (verb) lehaKHlif
exchange rate sha'ar KHalifin
excursion siyur
excuse: excuse me! (to get
  attention) sliKHa!
exit yetzi'a
expensive yakar
eye ayin
  eyes aynayim
  eye drops tipot aynayim

face panim
faint (unclear) metushtash
  (verb) lehit'alef
  to feel faint lehargish
  KHulsha
fair (funfair) yarid
  it's not fair zeh lo hogen
false teeth ktarim
family mishpaKHa
fan (ventilator) me'avrer
  (enthusiast) ma'aritz (m),
  ma'aritza (f)
  (sport) ohed (m), ohedet (f)
fan belt retzu'at ivrur
far: how far is ...? ma
  ha-merKHak le-...?
fare meKHir nesi'a
farm meshek
farmer KHaklai
fashion ofna
fast maher
fat (adj) shamen
father av
fax (noun) fax
  (verb) lishloaKH fax

feel (touch) laga'at
  I feel hot KHam li
  I feel like ... mitKHashek li ...
  I don't feel well ra li
feet kapot raglayim
felt-tip pen tush
ferry ma'aboret
fever KHom gavoha
fiancé arus
fiancée arusa
field sadeh
figs te'enim
filling (tooth) stima
  (sandwich etc) milui
film seret
filter filter
finger etzba
fire esh
  (blaze) srefa
fire extinguisher maKHshir kibui
  esh
firework zikuk
first rishon
first aid ezra rishona
first floor koma rishona
fish dag
fishing ladug
  to go fishing latzet ladug
fishing rod KHaka
fishmonger moKHer dagim
fizzy toses
flag degel
flash (camera) flesh
flat (level) shatuaKH
  (apartment) dira
flavour ta'am
flea pishpesh
  flea market shuk ha-pishpeshim
flight tisa
flip-flops kafkafim
flippers snapirim
flour kemaKH

flower peraKH
flu shapa'at
flute KHalil
fly *(noun: insect)* zvuv
  (verb: plane) latus
fog arafel
folk music musikat folklor
food oKHel
food poisoning har'alat kayva
foot kaf regel
football kaduregel
for bishvil, le-...
  for me bishvili
  what for? bishvil ma?
  for a week le-shavu'a
foreigner zar *(m)*, zara *(f)*
forest ya'ar
fork mazleg
fortnight shvu'ayim
fountain pen et nove'a
fourth revi'i
fracture shever
France tzorfat
free KHofshi
  (no cost) KHinam
freezer makpi
fridge mekarer
friend KHaver *(m)*, KHavera *(f)*
friendly yediduti
front: in front of ... lifnay ...
frost kfor
fruit *(singular)* pri
  (plural) payrot
fruit juice mitz payrot
fry letagen
frying pan maKHvat
full maleh
  I'm full ani maleh *(m)*/
  mele'a *(f)*
funnel *(for pouring)* mashpeKH
funny *(amusing)* matzKHik
  (odd) muzar

furniture rahitim

Galilee galil
  Sea of Galilee kineret
garage musaKH
garden gina
garlic shum
gay *(homosexual)* homosexual *(m)*,
  lesbit *(f)*
gear mahalaKH, hiluKH
gear lever yadit hiluKHim
gents *(toilet)* sherutay gvarim
Germany germania
get *(fetch)* lehavi
  have you got ...? yesh leKHa ...?
  (to a man)/laKH ..? *(to a woman)*
  to get the train litpos et
  ha-rakevet
  we get back tomorrow
  anaKHnu KHozrim maKHar
  to get something back lekabel
  be-KHazara
  to get in lehikanes
  (arrive) lehagi'a
  to get out latzet
  to get up *(rise)* lakum
gift matana
gin jin
girl yalda
  (older) na'ara
girlfriend KHavera
give latet
glad sameaKH
  I'm glad ani sameaKH *(m)*/
  smeKHa *(f)*
glass *(material)* zeKHuKHit
  (for drinking) kos
glasses mishkafayim
gloss prints hadpasot mavrikot
gloves kfafot
glue devek
goggles mishkafay sKHiya

gold zahav
good tov
good! tov me'od!
goodbye shalom
 (see you) lehitra'ot
government memshala
granddaughter neKHda
grandfather saba
grandmother savta
grandson neKHed
grapes anavim
grass desheh
Great Britain britania
green yarok
grey afor
grill gril
grocer (shop) makolet
ground floor komat karka
guarantee (noun) arvut
 (verb: promise) lehavtiaKH
guard shomer (m), shomeret (f)
guide book madriKH
guitar gitara
gun (rifle) roveh
 (pistol) ekdaKH

Haifa KHaifa
hair say'ar
haircut tisporet
hairdresser sapar (m), saparit (f)
hair dryer mayabesh say'ar
hair spray la-say'ar
half KHatzi
 half an hour KHatzi sha'a
hamburger hamburger
hammer patish
hand yad
handbag tik yad
handbrake ma'atzor yad
handkerchief mitpaKHat af
handle (door) yadit
handsome na'eh

hangover heng over
happy me'ushar
harbour namal
hard kasheh
hard lenses adashot maga kashot
hardware shop KHanut klay bayit
hat kova
have: I have a ... yesh li ...
 I don't have a ... ayn li ...
 can I have a ...? efshar
 lekabel ...?
 have you got a ...? yesh
 lekHa ...? (to a man)/laKH ..? (to a
 woman)
 I have to ... ani tzariKH(m)/tzriKHa
 (f) le-...
 I have to go now ani tzariKH (m)/
 tzriKHa (f) laleKHet aKHshav
hayfever elergia
he hu
head rosh
headache ke'ev rosh
headlights panasim kidmiyim
hear lishmo'a
hearing aid maKHshir shmi'a
heart lev
heart attack hetkef lev
heating KHimum
heavy kaved
Hebrew ivrit
heel akev
hello shalom
help (noun) ezra
 (verb) la'azor
 help! hatzilu!
her: it's her zot hi
 it's for her zeh bishvila
 give it to her ten (to a man)/tni
 (to a woman) la et zeh
 her house ha-bayit shela
 her shoes ha-na'alayim shela
 it's hers zeh shela

high gavoha
highway code KHukay ha-tnu'a
hill *(small)* giv'a
  (large) har
him: it's him zeh hu
  it's for him zeh bishvilo
  give it to him ten *(to a man)*/
  tni *(to a woman)* lo et zeh
hire liskor
  for hire le-haskara
his: his house ha-bayit shelo
  his shoes ha-na'alayim shelo
  it's his zeh shelo
history historia
hitch-hike la'atzor trempim
hobby taKHbiv
holiday *(break)* KHufsha
  (festival) KHag
Holland holand
Holy Land eretz ha-kodesh
honest yashar
honey dvash
honeymoon yeraKH dvash
horn *(car)* tzofar
  (animal) keren
horrible ayom
hospital bayt KHolim
hotel malon
hour sha'a
house bayit
how? ayKH?, ma?
  how do I get there? ayKH
  lehagi'a lesham?
  how is he? ma shlomo?
hungry: I'm hungry ani ra'ev
  (m)/re'eva *(f)*
hurry: I'm in a hurry ani
  memaher *(m)*/memaheret *(f)*
husband ba'al
  my husband/her husband
  ba'ali/ba'ala

I ani
ice keraKH
ice cream glida
ice cube kubiyat keraKH
ice lolly kartiv
if im
ignition hatzata
ill KHoleh
immediately miyad
impossible bilti efshari
in be-... , ba-...
  in English be-anglit
  in the hotel ba-malon
indicator itut
indigestion kilkul kayva
infection zihum
information mayda
injection zrika
injury petzi'a
ink dio
inner tube pnimit
insect repellent taKHshir neged
  yatushim
insomnia neduday shayna
insurance bituaKH
interesting me'anyen
interpret letargem
invitation hazmana
Ireland irland
Irish iri
Irishman iri
Irishwoman irit
iron *(noun)* maghetz
is: he is .../she is .../it is ...
  hu .../hi .../zeh ...
Islam islam
island 'ee
Israel yisra'el
Israeli *(man, adj)* yisra'eli
  (woman) yisra'elit
  the Israelis ha-yisra'elim
it zeh

114

itch *(noun)* gerud
  it itches zeh megared

jacket *(coat)* me'il
  (suit) ZHaket
jacuzzi jakuzi
Jaffa yafo
jam riba
jazz jaz
jealous mekaneh
jeans jins
jellyfish meduza
Jerusalem yerushalayim
Jesus yeshu
Jew yehudi *(m)*, yehudiya *(f)*
Jewish yehudi
jeweller *(shop)* KHanut
  taKHshitim
job *(work)* avoda
  (employment, project) job
jog *(verb)* larutz
  to go for a jog latzet le-joging
joke bdiKHa
Jordan *(river, state)* yarden
Jordanian *(man, adj)* yardeni
  (woman) yardenit
journey nesi'a
Judaism yahadut
jumper sveder
just: it's just arrived zeh karega
  higi'a
  I've just one left nish'ar li
  rak eKHad
  just two rak shnayim

key mafteaKH
kibbutz kibutz
kidney klaya
kilo kilo
kilometre kilometer
kitchen mitbaKH
knee bereKH

knife sakin
knit lisrog
know: I don't know ani lo yode'a
  (m)/yoda'at *(f)*
Koran kor'an
kosher *(noun)* kashrut
  (adj) kasher

label tavit
lace taKHara
laces *(of shoe)* sroKHim
ladies *(toilet)* shayrutay nashim
lake agam
lamb *(meat)* keves
lamp menora
lampshade ahil, nivreshet
land *(noun)* eretz
  (verb) linKHot
language safa
large gadol
last *(final)* aKHaron
  last week ha-shavu'a ha-aKHaron
  last month ha-KHodesh
  ha-aKHaron
  at last! sof sof!
late: it's getting late kvar
  me'uKHar
  the bus is late ha-otobus
  me'aKHer
laugh litzKHok
launderette maKHbesa
laundry *(place)* maKHbesa
  (dirty clothes) kvisa
laxative meshalshel
lazy atzlan
leaf aleh
leaflet alon
learn lilmod
leather or
Lebanese *(man, adj)* levanoni
  (woman) levanonit
Lebanon levanon

left *(not right)* smol
  there's nothing left lo nish'ar klum
left luggage locker shmirat KHafatzim
leg regel
lemon limon
lemonade limonada
length oreKH
lens adasha
less paKHot
lesson shi'ur
letter miKHtav
letterbox tayvat miKHtavim
lettuce KHasa
library sifriya
licence rishayon
life KHayim
lifeguard matzil *(m)*, metzila *(f)*
lift *(in building)* ma'alit
  could you give me a lift? efshar lekabel tremp?
light *(not heavy)* kal
  (not dark) bahir
lighter matzit
lighter fuel benzin le-matzit
light meter mad or
like: I like you ata motzeh *(to a man)*/at motzet *(to a woman)* KHen be'aynai
  I like swimming ani ohev *(m)*/ohevet *(f)* lisKHot
  it's like ... zeh kmo ...
lip salve sfaton neged yovesh
lipstick sfaton
liqueur liker
list reshima
litre liter
litter ashpa
little *(small)* katan
  it's a little big zeh ktzat gadol
  just a little rak ktzat

liver kaved
lobster lobster
lollipop sukaria al makel
long aroKH
  how long does it take? kama zman zeh yikaKH?
lorry masa'it
lost property office avaydot
lot: a lot harbeh
loud kol ram
loudly be-kol ram
lounge salon, traklin
  (hotel) lobi
love *(noun)* ahava
  (verb) le'ehov
lover me'ahev *(m)*, me'ahevet *(f)*
low namuKH
luck mazal
  good luck! be-hatzlaKHa!
luggage mit'an
luggage rack madaf le-tikim
lunch aruKHat tzohorayim

magazine ZHurnal
mail do'ar
make *(verb)* la'asot
make-up mayk ap, ipur
man ish, gever
manager menahel *(m)*, menahelet *(f)*
mango mango
map mapa
  a map of Jerusalem mapat yerushalayim
marble shayish
margarine margarina
market shuk
marmalade ribat tapuzim
married nasui *(m)*, nesu'a *(f)*
mascara maskara
mass *(church)* misa
mast toren

match *(light)* gafrur
  (sport) misKHak
material *(cloth)* bad
mattress mizron
maybe ulai
me: it's me zeh *(m)*/zot *(f)* ani
  it's for me zeh bishvili
  give it to me ten *(said to a man)*/tni *(said to a woman)* li
meal aruKHa
meat basar
mechanic meKHona'i
medicine trufa
Mediterranean ha-yam
  ha-tiKHon
meeting pgisha
melon melon
menu tafrit
message hoda'a
midday tzohorayim
middle: in the middle ba-'emtza
  the Middle East ha-mizraKH
  ha-tiKHon
  Middle Eastern mizraKH
  tiKHoni
midnight KHatzot
milk KHalav
mine: it's mine zeh sheli
mineral water mayim
  mineraliyim
minute daka
mirror re'i
Miss gveret
mistake ta'ut
  to make a mistake lit'ot
monastery minzar
money kesef
month KHodesh
monument andarta
moon yareaKH
moped katno'a
more od

morning boker
  in the morning ba-boker
mosaic psayfas
Moslem *(man, adj)* muslemi
  (woman) muslemit
mosque misgad
mosquito yatush
mother ima, em
motorbike ofano'a
motorboat sirat mano'a
motorway kvish mahir
mountain har
mouse aKHbar
moustache safam
mouth peh
move lazuz
  (house) la'avor dira
  don't move! lo lazuz!
movie seret
Mr mar
Mrs gveret
Ms gveret
much harbeh
  not much lo harbeh
  much better harbeh yoter tov
  much slower harbeh yoter le'at
mule pered
mum ima
museum musay'on
mushroom pitriya
music musika
musical instrument kli negina
musician musika'i *(m)*,
  musika'it *(f)*
  (player) nagan *(m)*, naganit *(f)*
mussels tzdafot
mustard KHardal
my: my bag hatik sheli
  my keys ha-mafteKHot sheli

nail *(metal)* masmer
  (finger) tziporen

nail file ptzira
nail polish lak la-tzipornayim
name shem
nappy KHitul
narrow tzar
Nazareth natzrat, natzeret
near leyad, al yad
  near the door leyad ha-delet
  near London al yad london
necessary naKHutz
necklace *(metal)* sharsheret
  (beads) maKHrozet
need *(verb)* lehitztareKH
  I need ... ani tzariKH *(m)*/
  tzriKHa *(f)* ...
  there's no need ayn tzoreKH
needle maKHat
negative *(photo)* negativ
neither: neither of them af
  eKHad mehem
  neither ... nor ... lo ... ve-lo ...
nephew aKHyan
never af pa'am lo
  I have never been to
  Jerusalem af pa'am lo hayiti
  be-yerushalayim
new KHadash
news KHadashot
newsagent moKHer itonim
newspaper iton
New Testament ha-brit
  ha-KHadasha
New Year's Day *(Jewish)* rosh
  ha-shana
  (Christian) rosh ha-shana
  ha-ezraKHit, silvester
New Zealand niu ziland
New Zealander *(man)* niu zilandi
  (woman) niu zilandit
next ha-ba
  next week ha-shavu'a ha-ba
  what next? ma hal'a?

nice neKHmad
niece aKHyanit
night laila
nightclub mo'adon laila
nightdress kutonet laila
night porter sho'er laila
no *(response)* lo
  there are no ... ayn ...
  I have no money ayn li kesef
noisy ro'esh
north tzafon
Northern Ireland tzfon irland
nose af
not lo
notebook maKHberet
nothing shum davar
novel roman
now aKHshav
nowhere shum makom
nudist nudist *(m)*, nudistit *(f)*
number mispar
number plate luKHit zihui
nurse aKH *(m)*, aKHot *(f)*
nut *(fruit)* egoz
  (for bolt) um

occasionally lif'amim
occupation kibush
  the occupied territories
  ha-shtaKHim ha-kvushim
octopus tamnun
of shel
office misrad
often le'itim krovot
oil shemen
  (for car) neft
ointment mishKHa, krem
OK beseder, o kay
old *(person)* zaken *(m)*, zkena *(f)*
  (object) yashan
  (ancient) atik
  the old city ha-'ir ha'atika

the Old Testament
ha-tanaKH
olive zayit
omelette KHavita
on *(on top of)* al
  (in operating mode) po'el
one eKHad
onion batzal
only rak
open *(verb)* liftoaKH
  (adj) patuaKH
opposite: opposite the hotel
mul ha-malon
optician optikai
or o
orange *(colour)* katom
  (fruit) tapuz
orange juice mitz tapuzim
orchestra tizmoret
ordinary *(normal)* ragil
our shelanu
  our hotel ha-malon shelanu
  it's ours zeh shelanu
out: he's out hu lo nimtza
  to get out latzet haKHutza
outside baKHutz
over me'al
  over there sham
overtake la'akof
oyster tzdafa

pack: pack of cards KHafisat
klafim
package KHavila
packet KHafisa
  a packet of ... KHafisat ...
padlock man'ul
page amud
pain ke'ev
paint *(noun)* tzeva
pair zug
pale KHiver

Palestine palestina, falastin
  (referring to the Land of Israel)
eretz yisrael
Palestinian *(man, adj)* palestinai,
falastini
  (woman) palestina'it, falastinit
Palestinians palestina'im,
falastinim
palm tree dekel
pancake pankayk
paper niyar
paracetamol akamol
parcel KHavila
pardon? sliKHa?
parents horim
park *(noun)* park
  (verb) laKHanot
parsley petrozilia
party *(celebration)* mesiba
  (group) kvutza
  (political) miflaga
passenger nose'a *(m)*, nosa'at *(f)*
Passover pesaKH
passport darkon
pasta pasta
path shvil
pavement midraKHa
pay leshalem
peace shalom
peach afarsek
peanuts botnim
pear agas
pearl pnina
peas afuna
pedestrian holeKH regel *(m)*,
holeKHet regel *(f)*
peg *(clothes)* mitleh
pen et
pencil iparon
pencil sharpener meKHaded
penfriend KHaver la-'et *(m)*,
KHavera la-'et *(f)*

peninsula KHatzi 'ee
penknife olar
people anashim
pepper pilpel
peppermints sukaryot menta
per: per night le-laila
perfect mushlam
perfume bosem
perhaps ulai
perm permanent
petrol delek
petrol station taKHanat delek
photograph *(noun)* tatzlum
  (verb) letzalem
photographer tzalam *(m)*,
  tzalemet *(f)*
phrase book siKHon
piano psanter
pickpocket kayas
picnic piknik
piece KHatiKHa
pillow karit
pilot tayas
pin sika
pine *(tree)* oren
pineapple ananas
pink varod
pipe *(for smoking)* mikteret
  (for water) tzinor
pistachio nuts fistuk KHalabi
pizza pitza
place makom
plant tzemaKH
plaster *(for cut)* plaster
plastic plastik
plastic bag sakit nylon
plate tzalaKHat
platform ratzif
play *(theatre)* maKHazeh
please bevakasha
plug *(electrical)* teka
  (sink) pkak

pocket kis
poison ra'al
police mishtara
policeman shoter
police station taKHanat mishtara
politics politika
pomegranate rimon
poor ani *(m)*, aniya *(f)*
  (bad quality) ra
pop music musikat pop
pork basar lavan
port *(harbour)* namal
porter *(for luggage)* sabal
  (hotel) sho'er
possible efshari
post *(noun)* do'ar
  (verb) lishloaKH
post box tayvat do'ar
postcard gluya
poster poster
postman davar
post office snif do'ar
potato tapuaKH adama
poultry off
pound *(money)* lira
  (weight) livra
powder avka
pram eglat tinok
prawn shrimp
pretty *(beautiful)* yafeh
  (quite) day
priest komer
print lehadpis
printer madpeset
private prati
problem be'aya
  what's the problem? ma
  ha-be'aya?
Protestant protestanti *(m)*,
  protestantit *(f)*
public *(noun)* tzibur
  (adj) tziburi

pull limshoKH
puncture pancher
purple sagol
purse arnak
push lidKHof
pushchair eglat yeladim
pyjamas pijama

quality ayKHut
quay ratzif
question she'ela
queue *(noun)* tor
  (verb) la'amod ba-tor
quick *(adj)* mahir
  quick! maher!
quiet *(adj)* shaket
  quiet! sheket!
quite *(fairly)* dai
  (fully) me'od

rabbi rav
radiator radyator
radio radio
railway line mesilat rakevet
rain geshem
raincoat me'il geshem
raisins tzimukim
rare *(uncommon)* nadir
  (steak) na
rat KHulda
razor blades sakinay giluaKH
read likro
reading lamp menorat kri'a
ready muKHan
rear lights orot aKHoriyim
receipt kabala
receptionist pkid kabala *(m)*,
  pkidat kabala *(f)*
record *(music)* taklit
  (sporting etc) si
record player patefon
record shop KHanut taklitim

red adom
refreshments kibud
registered letter miKHtav rashum
relative karov *(m)*, krova *(f)*
relax lanuaKH
religion dat
remember lizkor
  I don't remember ani lo
  zoKHer *(m)*/zoKHeret *(f)*
rent *(verb)* liskor
  rent out lehaskir
reservation hazmana
rest *(remainder)* ha-yeter
  (relax) lanuaKH
restaurant mis'ada
return *(come back)* laKHazor
  (give back) lehaKHzir
return ticket kartis haloKH va-shov
rice orez
rich ashir
right *(correct)* naKHon
  (direction) yamin
ring *(to call)* letzaltzel
  (wedding etc) taba'at
ripe bashel
river nahar
road *(main)* kvish
  (street, urban road) reKHov
rock *(large)* sela
  (small) even
  (music) rok
roll *(bread)* laKHmanya
roof gag
room KHeder
  (space) merKHav, makom panui
rope KHevel
rose vered
round *(circular)* agol
  it's my round aKHshav tori
rowing boat sirat meshotim
rubber *(eraser)* maKHak
  (material) gumi

rubbish ashpa
ruby *(stone)* margalit
rucksack tarmil gav
rug *(mat)* shatiaKH
  (blanket) smiKHa
ruins KHoravot
ruler *(for drawing)* sargel
rum rum
run *(verb)* larutz
runway maslul

Sabbath shabat
sad atzuv
safe batuaKH
  is it safe? zeh batuaKH?
safety pin sikat bitaKHon
sailing boat mifrasit
salad salat
salami naknik salami
sale *(at reduced prices)*
  meKHira
salmon salmon
salt melakH
same oto ha-...
  the same dress ota ha-simla
  the same people otam
  ha-anashim
  same again please shuv oto
  ha-davar, bevakasha
sand KHol
sandals sandalim
sand dunes KHolot
sandwich sendvich
sanitary towels taKHboshot
  intimiyot
sauce rotev
saucepan maKHvat
sauna sauna
sausage naknik
say lomar
  what did you say? ma amarta
  (to a man)/amart? *(to a woman)*

how do you say ... (in Hebrew)?
  ayKH omrim (be-'ivrit) ...?
scarf tza'if
  (head) mitpaKHat rosh
school bayt sefer
scissors misparayim
Scot *(man)* scoti
  (woman) scotit
Scotland scotland
Scottish scoti
screw boreg
screwdriver mavreg
sea yam
seafood payrot yam
seat moshav
seat belt KHagorat betiKHut
second *(of time)* shniya
  (in series) sheni
security bitaKHon
  security forces koKHot
  ha-bitaKHon
see lir'ot
  I can't see ani lo ro'eh *(m)*/ro'a *(f)*
  I see *(understand)* ani mevin *(m)*/
  mevina *(f)*
sell limkor
sellotape® niyar devek
separate nifrad
separated be-nifrad
serious retzini
serviette mapit
several kama
sew litpor
shampoo shampo
shave: to have a shave
  lehitgaleaKH
shaving foam ketzef giluaKH
shawl shal
she hi
sheet sadin
shell tzedef
sherry sheri

ship sfina
shirt KHultza
shoe laces sroKHay na'alayim
shoe polish mishKHat na'alayim
shoes na'alayim
shop KHanut
shopping kniyot
  to go shopping la'asot kniyot
short katzar
shorts miKHnasayim ktzarim
shoulder katef
shower (bath) miklaKHat
  (rain) geshem
shrimp shrimp
shutter (camera) miKHseh adasha
  (window) tris
sick (ill) KHoleh
  I feel sick ra li
side (edge) tzad, katzeh
sidelights orot tzad
sights (tourist) mar'ot
silk meshi
silver kesef
simple pashut
sing lashir
single (one) yaKHid
  (unmarried) ravak (m), ravaka (f)
single room KHeder le-yaKHid
sister aKHot
skid (verb) lehaKHalik
skin cleanser taKHshir nikui
  la-or
skirt KHatza'it
sky shamayim
sleep (noun) shayna
  (verb) lishon
  to go to sleep laleKHet lishon
sleeping bag sak shayna
sleeping pill kadur shayna
slippers na'alay bayit
slow (adj) iti
small katan

smell (noun) reyaKH
  (verb) lehariaKH
smile (noun) KHiyuKH
  (verb) leKHayeKH
smoke (noun) ashan
  (verb) le'ashen
snack KHatif
  (light meal) aruKHa kala
snorkel shnorkel
snow sheleg
so kol kaKH
  (thus) kaKH
  so good kol kaKH tov
  not so much lo kol kaKH harbeh
soaking solution (for contact
  lenses) tmisat hashraya
  le-adashot
socks garbayim
soda water soda
soft lenses adashot rakot
soldier KHayal (m), KHayelet (f)
somebody mishehu (m), mishehi (f)
somehow ayKHshehu
something mashehu
sometimes lif'amim
somewhere ayfo shehu
son ben
song shir
sorry: I'm sorry ani mitzta'er
  (m)/mitzta'eret (f)
  sorry! sliKHa!
soup marak
south darom
South Africa drom afrika
South African (man, adj) drom
  afrikai
  (woman) drom afrikait
souvenir mazkeret
spade (shovel) et
  (cards) yahalom
spanner mafteaKH bragim
spares KHalafim

123

spark(ing) plug matzat
speak ledaber
  do you speak ...? ata
  medaber ...? *(to a man)*/at
  medaberet ...? *(to a woman)*
  I don't speak Hebrew ani lo
  medaber *(m)*/medaberet *(f)*
  ivrit
speed mehirut
speed limit mehirut muteret
speedometer mad mehirut
spider akavish
spinach tered
spoon kaf
sport sport
sprain neka
spring *(mechanical)* kfitz
  (season) aviv
stadium itztadyon
staircase/stairs madregot
stamp bul
stapler shadKHan
star koKHav
  (film) koKHav kolno'a *(m)*,
  koKHevet kolno'a *(f)*
start *(verb)* lehatKHil
station taKHana
statue pesel
steak stayk
steal lignov
  it's been stolen zeh nignav
steering wheel hegeh
steward dayal
stewardess dayelet
sting *(noun)* akitza
  (verb) la'akotz
stockings garbiyonim
stomach beten
stomach ache ke'ev beten
stop *(verb)* la'atzor
  (bus stop) taKHanat otobus
  stop! atzor!

storm se'ara
strawberry tut
stream naKHal
street reKHov
string *(cord)* KHut
  (guitar etc) maytar
student student *(m)*, studentit *(f)*
stupid tipesh
suburbs parvarim, shKHunot
sugar sukar
suit *(noun)* KHalifa
  (verb) lehat'im
  it suits you zeh mat'im
suitcase mizvada
sun shemesh
sunbathe lehishtazef
sunburn kviyat shemesh
sunflower seeds KHamanyot
sunglasses mishkafay shemesh
sunny: it's sunny ha-shemesh
  zoraKHat
suntan shizuf
suntan lotion shemen shizuf
supermarket supermarket
supplement tosefet
sure: are you sure? ata batuaKH?
  (to a man)/at betuKHa? *(to a*
  woman)
  sure! betaKH!, bevadai!
surname shem mishpaKHa
sweat *(noun)* zay'a
  (verb) lehazi'a
sweatshirt svetshert
sweet *(not sour)* matok
  (candy) mamtak
swim lisKHot
swimming costume beged yam
swimming pool brayKHat sKHiya
switch meteg
  to switch on lehadlik
  to switch off lekHabot
synagogue bayt kneset

Syria surya
Syrian *(man, adj)* suri
  (woman) surit

table shulKHan
tablet kadur
take lakaKHat
take-away tayk eway
take off *(of plane)* lehamri
talcum powder talk
talk *(noun)* siKHa
  (verb) ledaber
tall gavoha
tampon tampon
tangerine mandarina
tap berez
tea teh
telegram mivrak
telephone *(noun)* telefon
  (verb) letalpen
telephone box ta telefon
telephone call siKHat telefon
television televizya
temperature temperatura
tent ohel
tent peg yated
than: better than ... yoter tov
  me'asher ...
thank *(verb)* lehodot
  thanks toda
  thank you toda raba
that: that bus ha-otobus
  ha-hu
  that man ha-ish ha-hu
  that woman ha-isha ha-hi
  what's that? ma zeh?
  I think that ... ani KHoshev
  (m)/KHoshevet *(f)* she-...
their: their room ha-KHeder
  shelahem *(m)*/shelahen *(f)*
  their books ha-sfarim
  shelahem *(m)*/shelahen *(f)*

it's theirs zeh shelahem *(m)*/
  shelahen *(f)*
them: it's for them zeh hem *(m)*/hen *(f)*
  it's for them zeh bishvilam
  (m)/bishvilan *(f)*
  give it to them latet et zeh
  lahem *(m)*/lahen *(f)*
then az
there sham
  there is/are ... yesh ...
  is/are there ...? yesh ...?
thermos flask termos
these: these things ha-dvarim
  ha-'eleh
  these are mine 'eleh sheli
they hem *(m)*, hen *(f)*
thick aveh
  (liquid) samiKH
thin *(person)* razeh *(m)*, raza *(f)*
  (object) dak
  (liquid) dalil
think laKHashov
  I think so ani KHoshev *(m)*/
  KHoshevet *(f)* kaKH
  I'll think about it aKHshov al
  zeh
third shlishi
thirsty: I'm thirsty ani tzameh *(m)*/
  tzme'a *(f)*
this: this bus ha-otobus ha-zeh
  this man haish ha-zeh
  this woman ha-isha ha-zo
  what's this? ma zeh?
  this is Mr ... zeh mar ...
  this is Ms ... zo gveret ...
those: those things ha-dvarim
  ha-hem
throat garon
throat pastilles kaduray metzitza
through dereKH
thunderstorm sufat re'amim
ticket kartis

tie *(noun)* aniva
  (verb) likshor
time zman
  what's the time? ma ha-sha‘a?
timetable luaKH zmanim
tin *(can)* kufsat shimurim
tin-opener potKHan kufsa‘ot
tip *(money)* tip
  (end) katzeh
tired ayef
  I feel tired ani ayef *(m)/*
  ayefa *(f)*
tissues tishu
to: to England le-anglia
  to the station la-taKHana
  to the doctor la-rofeh
toast tost
tobacco tabak
today hayom
together (be-)yaKHad
toilet shayrutim
toilet paper niyar to‘alet
tomato agvanya
tomato juice mitz agvanyot
tomorrow maKHar
tongue lashon
tonic water may tonic
tonight ha-laila
too *(also)* gam
  (excessive) midai
  too hot KHam midai
tooth shen
toothache ke‘ev shinayim
toothbrush mivreshet shinayim
toothpaste mishKHat shinayim
torch panas
tour siyur
tourist tayar *(m)*, tayeret *(f)*
tourist office lishkat mayda
  le-tayarim
towel magevet
tower migdal

town ir
town hall bayt iriya
toy tza‘atzu‘a
toy shop KHanut tza‘atzu‘im
track suit trayning
tractor traktor
tradition masoret
traffic tnu‘a
traffic jam pkak tnu‘a
traffic lights ramzorim
trailer nigrar
train rakevet
translate letargem
transmission *(for car)* tayvat
  hilukHim
travel agency soKHnut nesi‘ot
traveller's cheque travelers chek
tray magash
tree etz
trousers miKHnasayim
try lenasot
tunnel minhara
Turkey turkia
tweezers pintzeta
typewriter meKHonat ktiva
tyre tzamig

umbrella mitriya
uncle dod
under mitaKHat
underground rakevet taKHtit
underpants taKHtonim
understand lehavin
  I don't understand ani lo mevin
  *(m)/*mevina *(f)*
underwear bgadim taKHtonim
university universita
unmarried lo nasui *(m)/*lo nesu‘a *(f)*
until ad
unusual *(special)* mayuKHad
  (out of ordinary) bilti shigrati
up lemala

upwards klapay <u>mala</u>
urgent da<u>kh</u>uf
us: it's us zeh ana<u>kh</u>nu
  it's for us zeh bishvilenu
  give it to us ten *(said to a man)*/tni *(said to a woman)* et zeh lanu
use *(noun)* shimush
  (verb) lehishtamesh
  it's no use zeh <u>kh</u>asar sikui
useful shimushi
usual ragil
usually bedere<u>kh</u> klal

vacancy *(room)* makom panui
vacuum cleaner sho'ev avak
vacuum flask termos
valley emek
valve shastom
vanilla vanil
vase kad
veal bsar egel
vegetables yerakot
vegetarian *(person)* tzim<u>kh</u>oni *(m)*, tzim<u>kh</u>onit *(f)*
vehicle kli re<u>kh</u>ev
very me'od
view mar'eh, nof
viewfinder aynit
villa vila
village kfar
vinegar <u>kh</u>ometz
violin kinor
visa viza
visit *(noun)* bikur
  (verb) levaker
visitor *(guest)* orea<u>kh</u> *(m)*, ora<u>kh</u>at *(f)*
  (tourist) mevaker *(m)*, mevakeret *(f)*
vitamin tablet ka<u>dur</u> vitamin

vodka vodka
voice kol

wait *(verb)* le<u>kh</u>akot
  wait! <u>kh</u>akeh! *(to a man)*/<u>kh</u>aki! *(to a woman)*
waiter meltzar
  waiter! sli<u>kh</u>a!
waiting room <u>kh</u>adar hamtana
waitress meltzarit
  waitress! sli<u>kh</u>a!
Wales wayls
walk *(noun: stroll)* tiyul
  (verb: walk) lale<u>kh</u>et
  (stroll) letayel
  to go for a walk lale<u>kh</u>et letayel
walkman® wokmen
wall *(of house)* kir
  (of city, castle) <u>kh</u>oma
  the Wailing Wall ha-kotel hama'aravi
wallet arnak
war mil<u>kh</u>ama
wardrobe melta<u>kh</u>a
warm <u>kh</u>am
was: I was hayiti
  he was hu haya
  she was hi haita
  it was zeh haya
washing powder avkat kvisa
washing-up liquid sabon kelim
wasp tzir'a
watch *(noun)* sha'on
  (verb) litzpot
water mayim
waterfall mapal mayim
wave *(noun)* gal
  (verb) lenafnef
we ana<u>kh</u>nu
weather mezeg ha-avir
wedding <u>kh</u>atuna
week shavu'a

welcome: you're welcome
  (don't mention it) al lo da<u>v</u>ar
wellingtons magafay gumi
Welsh *(man, adj)* welshi
  (woman) <u>welsh</u>it
were: we were ha<u>y</u>inu
  you were *(singular)* ha<u>y</u>ita *(to a man)*/ha<u>y</u>it *(to a woman)*
  (plural) ha<u>y</u>item *(to men)*/ha<u>y</u>iten *(to women)*
  they were hem ha<u>y</u>u
west ma'arav
wet ratu<u>v</u>
what? ma?
wheel galgal
wheelchair kise<u>h</u> galga<u>l</u>im
when? matai?
where? ay<u>f</u>o?
which? ay<u>z</u>eh? *(m)*, ay<u>z</u>o? *(f)*, aylu? *(plural)*
whisky <u>v</u>iski
white lavan
who? mi?
why? lama?
wide ra<u>KH</u>av
wife isha
  my wife ishti
  his wife ishto
wind <u>r</u>ua<u>KH</u>
window <u>KH</u>alon
windscreen shimsha kidmit
wine <u>y</u>ayin
wine list tafrit <u>y</u>aynot
wing *(of plane)* kana<u>f</u>
with im
without bli
woman isha
wood *(material)* etz
wool <u>tz</u>emer

word mila
word processor me'a<u>b</u>ed tamlilim
work *(noun)* avo<u>d</u>a
  (verb) la'a<u>v</u>od
worse <u>y</u>oter garu'a
wrapping paper ni<u>y</u>ar ariza
wrist <u>p</u>erek yad
writing paper ni<u>y</u>ar kti<u>v</u>a
wrong lo na<u>KH</u>on

year shana
yellow <u>tz</u>aho<u>v</u>
yes ken
yesterday etmol
yet od
  not yet od lo
yoghurt <u>y</u>ogurt
you *(singular)* ata *(to a man)*/at *(to a woman)*
  (plural) atem *(to men or mixed group)*/aten *(to women)*
your *(singular)* shel<u>KH</u>a *(to a man)*/shela<u>KH</u> *(to a woman)*
  (plural) shela<u>KH</u>em *(to men or mixed group)*/shela<u>KH</u>en *(to women)*
  your shoes ha-na'ala<u>y</u>im shel<u>KH</u>a *(to a man)*/shela<u>KH</u> *(to a woman)*
  your book ha-se<u>f</u>er shel<u>KH</u>a *(to a man)*/shela<u>KH</u> *(to a woman)*
yours: is this yours? zeh shel<u>KH</u>a *(to a man)*/shela<u>KH</u>? *(to a woman)*
youth hostel a<u>KH</u>sanyat no'ar

Zionism tziyonut
Zionist *(man, adj)* tziyoni
  (woman) tziyonit
zip ro<u>KH</u>san
zoo gan <u>KH</u>ayot

Compiled by
Lexus Ltd
with
Fania Oz-Salzberger and Roberta Rosen-Kerler

Facts and figures given in this book were
correct when printed. If you discover any
changes, please write to us.

Set in 9/9 Plantin Light by
Typesetters Ltd, Hertford.
Printed in Great Britain by
HarperCollins Manufacturing, Glasgow.

Hugo's Simplified System

Hebrew
Phrase Book

Hugo's Language Books Limited